AWAKENING COUNSEL

A Practical Guide to Creating the Life You Want to Live

by

JIM WAWRO

AWAKENING COUNSEL
A Practical Guide to Creating the Life You Want to Live

ISBN: 978-0615660165
Copyright © 2012 by Jim Wawro

All rights reserved. No part of this book may be reproduced in any form or by any electronic or mechanical means, including information storage and retrieval systems—except in the case of brief quotations embodied in critical articles or reviews—without permission in writing from the author.

Dedication

For all who struggle to become who they really are.

CONTENTS

Opening Statement........................1
Chapter 1
  What's the Hold Up? 3
Chapter 2
  Sonny................................6
Chapter 3
  Thunderbird.........................14
Chapter 4
  Wedding Bell Blues..................19
Chapter 5
  Mirror Image........................23
Chapter 6
  Courting Intuition 26
Chapter 7
  It's in the Cards 39
Chapter 8
  The Teacher Appears.................46
Chapter 9
  We the People.......................73
Chapter 10
  Polonia.............................91
Chapter 11
  Healing 117
Chapter 12
  Thanksgiving in San Francisco......134
Chapter 13
  Oh Lord, Won't You Buy Me a Mercedes-Benz 151
Chapter 14
  A Happy Accident 165
Closing................................174
BIBLIOGRAPHY...........................184
ACKNOWLEDGMENTS........................187
ABOUT THE AUTHOR.......................189
ALSO BY THE AUTHOR.....................190

OPENING STATEMENT

"Know thyself."—*Oracle of Delphi temple inscription*

I WROTE THIS BOOK because I have discovered three things worth sharing—how to know what you want, how to get what you want, and how to heal in nearly any situation.

For many years, I practiced in one of the world's largest law firms as a civil litigation lawyer applying the laws of the land. During that time, I began to notice that there were other laws—unwritten, universal laws—that applied to everyone, just as surely as the law of gravity. This book is a chronicle of how I discovered what three of those laws are and how anyone can use them to start enjoying a more fulfilled, happy, and healthy life.

What are the unwritten, universal laws? Although there are many such laws that I know little about, this book focuses on just three about which I have learned something: the law of intuition, the law of manifestation, and the law of healing.

Where can one find out about these unwritten, universal laws? There are many ways in which such laws are quietly revealed to us: by teachers, from both ancient and modern texts, in intuitive insights, from seemingly "chance" encounters with others, through life's experiences, in dreams, and if we're very lucky, by mentors who care enough about us to tell us the truth. This book explores all of these sources.

Who can apply these laws and put them into practice? Anyone with an open mind can discover and use the three unwritten, universal laws this book covers to *know* what they really want, to *get* what they want, and to *heal* in just about any situation.

Why should you want to invoke these laws? To dramatically improve the quality of your personal and professional life! For a greater sense of fulfillment and joy! For better relationships with others! For a renewed sense of physical, emotional, and spiritual health! In other words, by way of the simple shift of your perceptions and beliefs described in this book, the limitless power of universal law can assist you in leading a life in which: a) your most heartfelt desires crystallize for you; b) you begin to manifest these "dreams" into reality; and c) healing becomes commonplace in your life.

Bold claims? Read these fourteen stories about moments in my life; try the Closing's short exercises on how to invoke each of the three laws; and judge for yourself whether I've made my case to your satisfaction.

If you are satisfied, put the fire of your own desire into any one—or all three—of these laws, and watch the power of the universe come alive!

CHAPTER ONE

WHAT'S THE HOLD UP?

"The only tyrant I accept in this world is the 'still small voice' within." —*Mahatma Gandhi*

It happened just as the sun was setting on a rainy southern California afternoon. I had left work early that day to pick up Halloween costumes in Hollywood. As I drove up to our small apartment building, I clicked the remote to open the street-level garage door and slowly drove in.

I got out of the car and opened the back door to collect the costumes. As the heavy garage door began to automatically slide closed, I sensed movement to my right and looked up to see someone running from the sidewalk into the garage. I couldn't see the figure clearly because "it" was backlit by the setting sun. When the figure turned slightly, though, I caught the glimpse of a pistol and heard the sound of a slide being racked, pumping a bullet into the pistol's firing chamber. I saw from his profile that he was a man in his mid-20s, about 5'8" tall (smaller than I), wearing Converse All Star sneakers and a kerchief pulled up around his nose, disguising his face like a train robber from an old Hollywood Western.

With a curse, he ran toward me and demanded the gold Rolex I was wearing. I was very alert; but, somewhat to my surprise, I was quite calm, as if I were merely watching the scene unfold. He cursed again, and by this time, he was standing next to me near the open rear door of my car.

"Give me the fucking watch."

I took the Rolex off and handed it to him, thinking it curious that he repeatedly used the slang for lovemaking to convey menace.

"Lie down in the back of the car," he said, motioning with the pistol.

Now this was something unexpected. *Does he want to shoot me?* I thought to myself. *I'd better do something about it, right now, if this guy wants to kill me, before he has me in a position where I can't overpower him, before he has time to pull the trigger.* The instinct flashed through my entire body: Fight.

But almost immediately I got a strong, peaceful, inner feeling, which conveyed, "Do what he asked. He just wants to make a clean getaway." I deliberately hesitated for a fraction of a second: *Do I try to overpower him, or do I follow the inner feeling and take the chance that he's not going to kill me?*

And he knew I was thinking it over: "I said lie down in the back of the fucking car!"

I decided to follow my inner feeling and did as he asked. Suddenly, he just ran away.

I sat up, completely unhurt, oddly relieved that the garish Rolex was out of my life. I also began to feel compassion for a young man whose brutish, and probably short, stay on this planet had to be supported by armed robbery. What's his life got to be like? The shock and emotion of the event began to ebb quickly away as I realized that I had just bet my life on that inner feeling. And I had won the bet.

As I sat in the back of the car, I began to think about how I had come to put so much trust in my inner voice, and I realized that it had probably all started the day that Sonny, my mentor, died.

CHAPTER TWO

SONNY

"Dream Catcher, send me a dream."—Robby Romero, Jim Wawro, et al. songwriters: "Dream Catcher," from the album *Hidden Medicine*

"Boom out!"

"What?" I asked.

"Put the car in drive, hit the gas, and boom out! Get us the hell out of here, before I croak from this heat!"

That was Sonny, my uncle Walter. He was my father's younger brother by nine years and the sixth of their parents' eight children. But he was only fifteen years older than I was—too old to be the older brother I never had, but too young to act like my father. His family called him "Sonny," and he always answered to it good-naturedly, even though he invariably introduced himself as "Walt." You never outgrow a nickname in a big family—your brothers and sisters still call you "Sonny" when you are 60 and they are 70, even though you're 6'4" tall, weigh 260 pounds, and have a wife and six children of your own.

But to me he was "sunny"—a great blast of energy, light, intelligence, and wit. Although I never stopped to think about it at the time, the feeling between us was mutual. I liked his irreverent humor, and he liked mine. I remember my family's visiting his growing family once in Flint, Michigan, when I was ten years old. As the adults talked, the children went outside to play baseball with the neighborhood children. The local kids were tough, distrusted outsiders, and wanted to make sure that any new kids knew the local rules. So when the biggest local kid heard me shouting baseball talk to his team's batters, he came right over and told me to stop it.

When I started again during his team's next at bats, the bully came over again: "I told you to stop, and I meant it. I don't want to hear another peep out of you."

Naturally, I uttered the only response I thought appropriate for that kind of directive: "Peep."

Fortunately, after my first warning from the local bully, my cousins had run to fetch Sonny, who arrived just in time to save me from a serious beating. He started to give me a lecture, but he was laughing too hard to pull it off. We understood each other from that moment on.

Sonny ("Uncle Walter" to me) worked as a traveling superintendent for a steel fabrication company, typically building conveyor systems in automobile assembly plants in the Northeast. He understood science, numbers, and the magical art of construction, making giant, useful, working machines out of I-beams, angle iron, bolts, welding rod, trolleys, and imagination. He could lay aerial steel jobs out in his mind, not on the floor like the other superintendents did, and plan bolt holes for steel pieces that actually fit together when the heavy steel pieces were hoisted thirty feet into the air by men on ladders.

He also had compassion for people's dreams and a passion to help them realize those dreams whenever he could. I saw him quietly help many people with a few dollars, a job, or a call to recommend; and he helped no one more than he helped me. He delighted in my dream, which, at thirteen years old, was to climb out of my dire financial circumstances by getting a first-class education when I was young and then becoming a lawyer. My plan for my dream was to attend the best private high school in my city and to pay for it through scholarships and by working two jobs during the school year. But Uncle Walter knew that the college and law school parts of my dream would cost more money than could be provided by a newspaper delivery route and a tree nursery job. So, when I was 16 and for the next eight summers after that, he had me travel with him and work with his steel construction crews. I made enough in his jobs to pay for my summer living expenses, school year room and board, and that portion of school tuition not covered by scholarships and loans. I also made more per hour in that job than I made per hour for several years as a lawyer.

What an experience those summers with Uncle Walter were! Because the twenty or so union workers on each of our steel fabrication jobs in different parts of the Northeast were all hired locally for each job, I got to experience the different communities of our many job sites through the eyes of the local residents. Uncle Walter and I worked during the day, starting each morning before work with a cup of coffee or tea and the local newspaper. We'd always open it at precisely 7:45 a.m. for our daily contest to see who could first get the answers to that day's "Jumble" puzzle. At night, we went out to a simple dinner at a local diner, visited the local sights, drove golf balls at a local driving range, played cards, or simply talked. He took great pains to teach me about life during those summers, and the curriculum I learned working with, and eventually supervising, steel construction workers was an interesting counter-point to the classical Latin and Greek education I was receiving during the school year.

And I also got to learn by example from Uncle Walter: have fun in the moment, don't take life too seriously, help people quietly when you can, solve problems to the best of your ability, and joke your blues away. I remember eating lunch on the job site in a helicopter factory one day. Uncle Walter was drinking from a milk carton, and an ironworker built like The Hulk walked by and said as he passed Uncle Walter, "Fuck a man who drinks milk." I thought, *Is this ironworker really trying to pick a fight over milk?* But we were both laughing so hard at the absurdity of the situation that the ironworker simply grunted and moved on.

Uncle Walter was my lifeline to get the dream I wanted, and I appreciated what he and his patient wife had done to help me. As I matured, we grew closer and consulted with each other over all major decisions we each faced in life. He came out to California to spend a day to listen to me tearfully go over the pros and cons of divorcing my first wife; and when the decision came about which parent would take responsibility for raising our child, he simply said, "He needs you now." And raise him I did. When Uncle Walter joined another company and could relocate to anywhere in the United

States reasonably close to a major airport, I interviewed him about what he wanted in a home base, researched the possibilities, and presented him with three alternatives. He picked my first choice and moved there with his family. He was the best man at my second marriage; and when one of his daughters had to have an operation because of an injury from a product defect, we visited her in the hospital regularly and found them a lawyer to prosecute her product defect action successfully.

Our relations with others were not always so perfect. My mother never liked Sonny because his humor could be "smart alecky." My father felt that Sonny competed with him for authority over me, a competition that apparently arose out of a brotherly wrestling match before I was born between Sonny (newly discharged from the Navy) and my father. Their wrestling had suddenly turned serious and ended up in Sonny's having to admit defeat out loud in front of the whole family, who had gathered to see what the commotion in Grandmother's kitchen was about. We both had had our difficulties with women and with successfully raising children into happy adults; but we liked and understood each other in ways that brought out the best in each of us.

For his 60th birthday, I surprised Uncle Walter with a fishing trip to Baja, California. We met with our wives at the Mexican Airlines check-in counter at LAX, and I can still see his smile begin as he realized that our meeting that day was not an accident, that it had all been arranged without his knowledge, and that he was about to have some days of fun. And fun it was: we explored the colonial town of Loreto, fished, visited the old San

Javier Jesuit mission, listened to mariachi music, lay on the beach, walked in the desert, told stories, and laughed a lot.

During one of our cab rides from the El Presidente hotel into town for dinner in Loreto, he turned to me and suddenly asked, "Will you forgive me?"

"For what?" I replied, but he wouldn't say. He had been my employer and, at times, was hard on me, but never mean. Perhaps I had been a pawn in his competition with my father, but it had allowed me to realize my dreams. Also, I *had* straightened things out with my father later anyway. I wondered what he was feeling so guilty about.

I asked again, "Forgive you for what?"

He wouldn't answer, so I just said: "I forgive you."

He said, "Thank you." And he wasn't kidding. It seemed to be something that he really wanted, and it seemed at that moment to give him an obvious peace. We quickly started to joke about something else and the trip went on. We never spoke of that moment again. I

occasionally look at a photograph I took of him on that trip, leaning against the stern of a fishing *panga*, obviously enjoying the warm breeze, the blue water of the Sea of Cortez in the background, beret on his head, and his face relaxed into a happy, unforced smile.

A year and a half later, I decided to take a Silva Mind Control course, figuring that the course could help me learn something about the mind's powers.

According to the promotional literature, the four-day Silva course, often given over two succeeding weekends, has been taken by over 4 million people worldwide. The course methodically shows its students how to consciously reach the theta brain wave stage, where the mind, though awake, is free to wander to other thoughts; as it does when, for example, a person is driving on a familiar freeway, jogging a daily route, or meditating.

The course emphasizes the importance of recording dreams because dreams occur in the theta brain wave stage when the mind is freelancing. The course teaches that, throughout history, it's been observed that human consciousness, while dreaming, can roam anywhere in "reality," can sometimes come upon surprisingly accurate information to solve problems, can view remotely, see the future, and know things unapproachable by the five waking senses.

At the end of that day's session, I was open to possibilities of the mind that I had never before considered, and I was determined to record all of my dreams that evening. I went to sleep that night, dreamed, and recorded the following dream when I awoke the next morning:

A formal (black tie) law firm function for lawyers only is being held at night, at the end of the driveway in the back of Uncle Walter's old house in New York. I do not want to attend; so I climb up onto the roof, using a sand pile up the backside of the house. Over on the other side, the roof is very steep. Someone (vaguely female and thirties, perhaps wearing a white shirt, not connected with the party) in the yard, near the steep side, is calling out for a child. I am thinking that climbing around on the roof is not a fun way to avoid the party.

I attended the next session of the Silva course the following day, and when I got home that evening, there was a message waiting for me on the answering machine to call Uncle Walter's youngest son. I called immediately and learned that Uncle Walter had died of a heart attack in Colorado at 3:15 p.m. that afternoon.

Perhaps I was open to the experience of clearly receiving a "dream message" about Uncle Walter because I was in the midst of taking the mind course; perhaps Uncle Walter's connection with me was that strong; perhaps my inner voice was giving me a signal to pursue my investigation of the mind. What I know for *sure* is that *something* communicated Uncle Walter's death to me in a dream 12 hours before it happened. And in that dream, I believe that I saw an angel from the other side calling for a child, calling for "Sonny" to come home.

Looking back on it, that was not the first time the universe spoke to me in pictures. The first time was when I was twelve years old.

CHAPTER THREE

THUNDERBIRD

"There are more things in heaven and earth, Horatio, than are dreamt of in your philosophy."—*Hamlet*, Act 1, Scene 5

ONE OVERCAST FALL DAY after a rainstorm, when I was twelve years old, I went out with my best friend, Jack, to tramp around in the wet forest with our bows and arrows. There was always something interesting to see in the forest, and Jack and I typically had a good time talking with each other while we explored. We rarely shot the arrows in the forest—in the dense forest, a flying arrow was soon, and irretrievably, lost in the undergrowth. We carried the bow and arrows for protection, I guess, or for the illusion of control. There were some scary creatures that used the forest. Once, as I was walking under a tree on my paper route in the predawn hours, a mountain lion screamed directly above me. Also, a huge wild boar charged past us once, and we often heard snakes slithering out of our way in the underbrush. Trust me: all of these experiences had a deep impact on us, challenging us both to keep coming back for more of what, apparently, we each really wanted: *more adventure*.

We were both a little bit scared and secretly proud of our mysterious forest. We had been taught in school that the forest was originally part of a much larger tract of land owned by Robert Morris, a signer of the Declaration of Independence and a financier of the American Revolution. The early settlers had logged and cleared much of the tillable land and eagerly sold off swaths of land unusable for farming to the railroad, which laid and maintained its tracks. For more than a hundred years, the railroad owners ignored the quarter-mile buffer zone on either side of its main line. The buffer zone then became a wild place, filled with mature second-growth hardwoods, elm and maple, and swamp, where no one went except for the few neighborhood children, like Jack and me. We occasionally ice-skated there during the winter, and explored there during the late spring and summer. Thus, since the time of the Indians, the land around my childhood home had been rural and, in the railroad buffer zone a quarter-mile south of my house, wild.

Across the road from our house was a fifty-acre wheat field, which butted up to the forest. Near to where the wheat field ended and the forest began, a single, large elm tree stood majestically, perhaps forty feet tall, with two large, upward-reaching limbs. From my front yard, then, there was an unobstructed view across the wheat field directly to the large elm.

As Jack and I poked around in the woods that day, we suddenly heard a loud squawking, as if two large creatures were battling or charging through the brush quite close to us. We notched our arrows and slowly backed away from the sound. Jack suddenly remembered that he had something to do back at his house and so we decided to leave the forest and its mysterious commotion. Jack walked back toward his house and I toward mine.

When I got home, I turned to look back casually at the forest, over the wheat field, out to the lone elm. There, on the right fork extending out over the wheat field, was a huge shape. Startled, I looked more closely and realized that the shape was of a bird, but the biggest bird that I had ever seen! Suddenly, it opened its wings and began a long, slow flap. I knew the lone elm tree well, and the slowly-flapping wings seemed as long as a substantial portion of the trunk of the old tree, perhaps twelve feet or more. As this flying monster gained altitude, two smaller birds circled its head, apparently pecking at the giant bird to drive it away from their nest. I watched the enormous bird slowly flap and glide along until it disappeared in the gray sky, heading in the direction of the Appalachian Mountains.

I ran excitedly into the house to tell my mother and father about the huge bird. They had seen large hawks, I knew, and even eagles occasionally flying in our skies; but *never* a bird with a 12-foot wingspan. Once they'd heard me gush about what I'd just seen, my mother suggested that we all get into the car and drive to the library to look at books with pictures of North American birds. One bird that seemed closest in shape and color to the bird I saw was the turkey vulture, but its maximum wingspan was listed in the book at only 6 feet, less than *half* of the size of the wingspan of the bird I saw.

I'm sure I talked about the bird non-stop for days and about whether the commotion Jack and I heard in the forest was the huge bird battling with some prey. But the bird had flown away; I never saw another one near our house, and I forgot the incident.

Forty years later, I was paying half-attention to a television program about unexplained phenomena, when the program began describing "thunderbirds," huge birds of Native American legend that were big enough to carry off children. The program had eyewitness interviews with a child who had been snatched and released by such a big bird in the late 1970s and footage of such a bird taken a few days later and 50 miles away by a former Marine combat photographer. The program ran the Marine's footage, and suddenly, I saw again the bird I had seen 40 years earlier!

The program theorized that large birds could ride the thermals that well up from the Gulf of Mexico and the Atlantic Ocean in two great rivers of air that sweep up the Mississippi River Valley and along the Appalachian Range, the places where the sightings of huge birds are occasionally seen. The strongest thermals are associated with turbulent weather, which is why sightings of huge birds are often connected with thunderstorms and why the Native Americans referred to the birds as "thunderbirds." An expert zoologist on the program said that the bird in the Marine's footage looked like a turkey vulture (as did the bird I saw) but that its size and wingspan (estimated by the Marine at 18-20 feet) were impossible to verify because of the absence of reliable indicators of scale in the footage. The zoologist went on to describe the largest bird known today as the Andean condor, with a 12-foot wingspan. There was another type of condor with a 25-foot wingspan in the fossil records, but it had gone extinct millions of years ago.

I recorded the television program, and I watch it from time to time. The Marine's footage of the huge bird brings back the memory of a similar giant bird I saw 20 years earlier than the Marine's record. I don't know exactly how big the huge bird was that I saw when I was 12, but I do feel blessed that Mother Nature singled me out to be one of the few people ever to have seen one of her best-kept secrets—a real "thunderbird."

Maybe that was the first time that the universe reached out to reveal to me something about what I had told myself I truly wanted. Maybe getting married was the second.

CHAPTER FOUR

WEDDING BELL BLUES

"Your mind knows only some things. Your inner voice, your instinct, knows everything. If you listen to what you know instinctively, it will always lead you down the right path."—*Henry Winkler*

"Get off my dress," she screeched, as the limousine rounded a corner on the way to the church.

I quickly moved to the other side of the limousine, so as not to put any thought of a wrinkle into a young woman's wedding day.

She was my first serious girlfriend and my first love, and I was her first. We had met on the first day of college and had remained together throughout our four years there. What had most attracted me to her was her apparent single-minded devotion to me. We planned that I would pursue further education after we were married, that she would work during the school years, and that I would work to support us during the summers. We thus tied our financial, emotional, and family futures together and planned on getting married.

My fiancée's mother had organized a big wedding for her only daughter, with a large wedding party, more than a hundred guests, and a traditional ceremony in the local New York City church where her family had attended services each week for the past fifty years. Guests were coming from my hometown three hundred miles away, the date was set, and the countdown began.

Exactly a week before our wedding day, I began to get the powerful feeling: "Don't do this." The feeling was not judgmental; it suggested no alternative courses of action; it was just *there*: "Don't do this."

I confided in my closest friends, who all counseled me that the feeling was just ordinary pre-marriage jitters, which many people went through. I thought about the tremendous upset that backing out now would cause to our relationship and to our plans. I was to start further schooling soon after the honeymoon. If I backed out now, my planned source of financial support would suddenly disappear. What would I do then? Following the feeling seemed impossible. Still, the feeling persisted: "Don't do this."

I confided in my fiancée about the feeling. "How could you do this to me?" she demanded. "What do I say to my family and friends?" She began crying and said, "I'll have to take rat poison."

Shocked by her response, I didn't raise the issue again.

All of the advice I had received, the planning I had done, the financial circumstance I was in, and the practicalities of the situation urged me to go through with it. Only the feeling, "Don't do this," compelled me not to. I thought it over for the rest of the week and finally decided to go through with the wedding. And that's how

I talked myself into marrying a woman to whom I was not suited.

There followed many years of trying to make the marriage work, years of mutual dissatisfaction, a child, a law school education for her, and further difficulties from trying to join irreconcilable forces peacefully. Then there was the emotionally-charged divorce, the financial toll, the inevitable damage to our beloved child, and the rough shaping of my life by cause and effect, like the sculpting of a statue with an ax.

Thirty years pass. The occasional migraines are increasing in frequency and intensity, and I have the feeling that my litigation practice in one of the world's largest law firms is soon going to end by my leaving that life by choice or by heart attack. But I have no suitable alternative way to spend my time and not enough money to stop working. *What do I do?* The answer I get—in the form of an intuitive feeling—is, "Walk out the door." I turn it over in my mind for several months, juxtaposing this feeling to "walk out the door" with the intellectual certainty that such an act is well-nigh impossible because I have no job, no prospects, no plan, and lots of anxiety.

But this time, I *follow the feeling*. I walk out the door. I decide to move to a small California mission town near the ocean and use my time to write *Listen to Your Inner Voice*, a book about the "still small voice." For the next six months, I work on the book, explore the Internet, go wine tasting, live on my dwindling savings, and worry a lot. Did I wonder during that time if I had made a big, stupid mistake? You bet.

The day comes when *Listen to Your Inner Voice* is written and on its way to the publishers. *What do I do now?* I wonder. The telephone rings. It's one of the partners in my best friend's small Los Angeles law firm.

"What are you doing? We have too many client matters and need help reviewing files and developing cases."

From that day on, for the next ten years, in the morning I read files, analyze cases, and interact with old colleagues on the telephone and through the Internet, without ever having to go to the office, deal with adversaries, or appear in court. In the afternoon, I enjoy life on California's coast.

Suddenly, the law work slows down and then stops. Again, I'm forced to reflect: *What do I do now for work and finances?* In several incidents of intuition, I get the feeling that I should take this slow time to write a book that mirrors what my experience has taught me about life. I listen to the feeling and begin to write my stories. When I get to the wedding bell story, the words of the episode seem to rush out onto the paper. I let the writing of the words wash my blues away. And I remember that even in my deepest funks, love was never very far away.

CHAPTER FIVE

MIRROR IMAGE

"At the touch of love everyone becomes a poet."
—*Plato*

Have you ever had a "disaster period" in your life? That time when your career is faltering, your relationships are an irritation, your cherished dreams seem childishly unrealistic, and you're getting fat? That time when you've tried everything to make something happen, and nothing does? When your soul cries out to whomever will listen, and no one will?

I have.

Then one day, when you've *stopped* asking for (or demanding) a miracle, the universe suddenly drops a flower in your hand. Your past clarity about what you truly want, your intention, feeling, expectation, and belief of having "it," and then that sense of finally letting go of it…all these bring forward that "gift" of something new. On that day, you begin to see in new ways; you become a poet again; and you start to get back up.

When we were sitting on your bed
Looking at each other in the mirror
(You naked; me nearly so),
I mused that we were so different.
"Because I'm Oriental?" you asked quickly
In your challenging but accepting way.
I looked again in the mirror
At your slender-waist-long-hair, deep-dark eyes,
Delicate brown body, and thought on
What you had said about the Caucasian,
The war, the camps, the Arkansas humidity,
The blank pages in my history books.
"No, because…" and I let it drift away,
Looking again in the mirror at my long limbs,
Blue-grey eyes, pallid skin, mussed hair,
Thinking on the contradictions
In what we are and how
We came to sit together here.
It is "yes" partly because in your mirror
We do look like we were cast
By a mold-maker who,
Having poured out a night sea-mist,
Tried next to cast from his mold
A desert morning.
It is "no" partly because
I live many lives,
You one Life;
Because I am a
Beached sea urchin, while you are
A sea anemone thriving
Beneath the crashing surf.
We let it pass into time

Unreconciled,
Each preferring to give the other
This quiet moment
Sitting on your bed
Looking at each other in the mirror.

CHAPTER SIX

COURTING INTUITION

"There is no substitute for reading the file."—*Anonymous*

"CASE NUMBER CV 0620-96, *Francisco v. Industrial Business Services*. Counsel, please state your appearances," the court clerk said, as he called our case for trial.

The lawyers for the various parties entered their formal appearances on the record, and the presiding judge asked, "Counsel, are there any pre-trial motions?"

We all answered, "Yes," and proceeded to present our pre-trial motions before jury selection began. The parties in the case were a plaintiff-worker injured on the job, his employer (a nation-wide food processing company), the employer's in-house worker's compensation risk manager, a worker's compensation insurance company, and a sole-practitioner doctor (my client).

The worker-plaintiff's case was that he was working in his job as a maintenance mechanic for the food processing company when he injured his back on the job. Under California's worker's compensation system at the time, a worker with the plaintiff's type of injury could return to work only under a doctor's supervision. The plaintiff was sent for review to my client, a young orthopedic surgeon in his first year of practice. After a medical examination and X-rays, the doctor gave the worker a "return to work order" worker's compensation form, which temporarily restricted the worker to "light duty," with a checked "expectation" that the restriction to "light duty" would become permanent. When the worker returned to the job with the "return to work order," the food processing company refused to permit the worker to return to the job because the job was strenuous and unsuitable for someone with a work restriction. The worker was out of work for many months and sustained financial damage because he was unable to work.

During the Worker's Compensation proceedings, a note from a temporary receptionist in the doctor's office was found in the doctor's file for the worker. The note was of a telephone call allegedly from the food processing company's in-house worker's compensation risk manager to the doctor about the worker and included the phrases:

"[T]he insurance company [w]ants him washed out."
"Wants you to handle it."
"Doesn't mind if it costs a couple of thousand."

Other evidence was developed during pre-trial discovery to the effect that the insurance company claims personnel thought that the food processing company was offering the claimant worker's compensation rehabilitation benefits "just to get rid of him." The plaintiff-worker and his wife were suing the defendants for millions of dollars in actual and punitive damages.

The doctor's defense was that the "light duty" restriction was medically appropriate because the patient had fractured facets in his vertebrae, that the doctor's medical opinion had been independently arrived at, and that the doctor had had no participation in what the employer did in barring the worker from further work. The food processing company and its in-house risk manager settled on the first day of trial, and the case proceeded before the empanelled jury against the insurance company and the doctor.

The trial continued through weeks of medical and other testimony. We were able to establish through the testimony and the personal diary of the doctor's temporary receptionist that she had likely only worked at the doctor's office, and had thus received the telephone call reflected in the handwritten note, on the day *after* the doctor had already given the worker the "return to work order" with the medical restriction. Hence, we argued, the doctor's medical restriction was correct, independently arrived at, and had been issued before the doctor knew anything about the employer's alleged intentions. Further, we argued that the doctor never knew what the employer ultimately did regarding the worker's status *and* that when doctors received comments like those in this case, they simply ignored the comments and instead gave their best professional medical opinion.

After nearly a month of trial, the plaintiffs' lawyer suddenly asked to speak with the judge out of the jury's presence, late one afternoon.

"Judge," the plaintiffs' lawyer said, "my investigator

went to the Worker's Compensation Board office where the originals of the doctor's forms are filed. He reported back to me that the original documents are full of erasures and, as he put it, 'little volcanoes' of Wite-Out that did not appear on the photocopies of the documents we were all using during the pre-trial and trial proceedings in the case. I've subpoenaed the documents to be delivered to your chambers tomorrow morning. Could Your Honor please call the Worker's Compensation Board office and confirm that the documents are to be here tomorrow, so that they can be examined by my questioned documents expert?"

"Any objections?" the judge asked the lawyers for the other parties.

No one said a word.

"All right," the judge said, "I'll call the Worker's Compensation office. I'm sure there will be no problem in getting the documents here tomorrow at 9:00 a.m., since that office is just across the quadrangle. The procedure we'll follow on this will be to have the plaintiffs' documents expert review the forms first, then anyone else can have their own documents expert look at the documents. The only thing is that all of the examiners who look at the documents must be available to testify about their conclusions to the jury later in the morning. Fair enough? Any questions?"

No one spoke.

"OK," the judge said, "I'll see everyone here tomorrow morning at 9:00 a.m."

"Thank you, Your Honor," we all said together and broke for the day.

Outside the courtroom, my client quickly pulled me

aside and said, "That didn't sound good at all. What's happening?"

"What the plaintiffs' lawyer is apparently going to try to show," I said, "is that the Worker's Compensation forms from your office were typed with your original diagnosis; then the telephone call came in from the employer asking for the medical restriction; and following that, someone erased the original diagnosis on the forms, Wited-out the erasures, and retyped the forms with the restrictive medical diagnosis that the other defendants wanted. That's his conspiracy theory, and he thinks the original documents will support it."

"My office would never do such a thing," the doctor said. "Besides, haven't we already shown through the temporary receptionist's diary that the call came in after the forms had already been sent in?"

"The evidence of the timing of the forms and the call is good, but the jury can disregard it if there's other contrary evidence in the case," I said, "and the plaintiffs' lawyer will try to show through the original documents with the Wite-Out on them that the diagnosis was, in fact, somehow changed."

"How is he going to do that?"

"He hopes, through a questioned documents expert."

"Is there such a thing? It doesn't sound very scientific to me."

"Well, as you know, the law allows a witness to testify if he has special knowledge or experience qualifying him, in the judge's opinion, to testify as an expert in his subject area. In the preliminary hearing, the judge will rule on whether the expert is qualified to testify, and I'm certain that he will be found qualified. The courts do allow questioned document experts to testify, even though their area of expertise is somewhat questionable—there's no degree granted for questioned documents study. But, over time, such experts have developed certain tests that the courts have found reliable enough to allow their testimony."

"Like what tests?"

"For subsequent changes to typed documents, the questioned documents experts have developed a very precise, see-through plastic or glass grid, lined out like a piece of graph paper. The see-through grid can be laid over a questioned document so that the original typing on the document fits exactly in the center of the little boxes. Any new typing that has been added to the document after the document has been taken out of the typewriter and rolled back in will not exactly line up with the original typing. The expert will then come to a conclusion about whether the typing on the page was done all at the same time or at different times, when the paper was rolled in and out of the typewriter."

"Can't the plaintiffs' lawyer just hire an expert who will say the typing was done on two different occasions, no matter what the grid shows?"

"Well, it's true with most expert witnesses that the lawyers can keep looking until they find the right one and then tell that witness exactly how to present their testimony if they're comfortable with defending it on cross-examination. However, questioned documents examiners are different."

"How so?"

"Because, unlike doctors or engineers, questioned documents experts do *not* have a primary profession to fall back on if something goes wrong in their witness work—testifying *is* their work. A questioned documents examiner's prospect of being hired for future jobs depends entirely on his reputation for accurate, unbiased work. Consequently, questioned documents experts insist upon 'calling them as they see them,' even if their testimony destroys the case of the side that paid them to testify."

"Are you sure about that?"

"Definitely. I've interviewed several of these experts for other cases, and they all start with the same warning to the lawyers—that they will not be swayed or told what to say, because their reputation is at stake. If they think the document changes are innocent, suspicious, or they just don't know one way or the other, they are going to say exactly that. Besides, there are only a handful of experts in this area, and the ones with the best reputations get all of the work. In the final analysis, there's also a safeguard—the examiner's testimony tomorrow has to be consistent with what the grid lines plainly show or else the judge won't let him testify to the jury."

"What are the grid lines going to show?"

"It's likely that the examiners will be able to testify tomorrow about whether or not the original typing and the corrections were done on the same roll of the paper into the typewriter."

"That's what I'm afraid of. My office uses temporary typists and medical document services to type batches of Worker's Compensation forms using IBM Selectric-type typewriters instead of computer printers. There are *many* possible explanations of how Wite-Out and typing changes came to be made on the forms. The typist could have taken the form out of the typewriter, realized that something was wrong on the form, rolled the form back into the typewriter, and made the correction."

"Well, if that happened, the questioned documents expert will probably be able to testify that the form had been rolled through the typewriter twice. That will be a powerful piece of circumstantial evidence against us, even if the typing and retyping by the temporary typist was completely innocent."

"And my career goes down the drain based on that?" the doctor asked.

"Of course, it's also possible that the typist realized that something was wrong on the form while it was still in the typewriter, rolled the form up a few spaces to be corrected without being removed from the typewriter, applied the Wite-Out, made the correction, and either rolled the completed form out of the typewriter or back into position to complete the form. That is a good possibility for a busy typist with dozens of forms to complete. None of the typists could remember, when we asked them during discovery, whether they had been the one who had actually typed the documents; but they all said that they often did their corrections while the paper was still in the typewriter. I'm not going to sugar-coat it, though—it's equally possible that the typist rolled the paper back into the machine a second time to do the corrections. The document examiners will likely catch that tomorrow and testify about it to the jury."

The doctor snorted, "Can't you object that this whole questioned document thing is just a lot of guesswork and that an innocent correction can be given a bad meaning?"

"Sure, we could object like crazy, and the judge, and later the jury, who have been watching us perform every day for the past month, will get the feeling that we're afraid of what the document examination shows. The judge will almost certainly admit the questioned documents examiners' testimony, no matter what objections we make. Then we're left with trying to explain away how the corrections could have been made innocently, even though the corrections were made *after* the paper was removed from the typewriter and sometime later reinserted to make the corrections.

"We could also do nothing," I continued, "and let the process play out while we remain silent; but that will likely communicate to the judge and the jury that we're nervous about what the questioned document examination shows. Any 'it could have been innocent' argument we make after that will appear weak.

"But," I said, "we can also take a *different* approach. We can confidently embrace the process, hire the best questioned documents examiner we can find on this short notice, fight to have his testimony admitted, and live with the result."

"What do we do?" the doctor asked.

"Ever since I started in this business, I have followed the trial lawyer's first rule: 'Never ask a question to which you do not already know the answer.' Here, we definitely do not know what the original documents are going to look like tomorrow morning or what any of the questioned documents experts are going to testify to the jury about the documents later in the day. And, by confidently embracing the process instead of objecting to it, we are clearly asking questions to which we do not know the answer. But we may have to take a risk here. Objecting or remaining silent will make it look like we think something's wrong or that we don't know whether something's wrong. Embracing the process will make it look like we're confident that no wrongdoing occurred; *but* the examiners may find that the forms were rolled through the typewriter twice, and we are left trying to explain that away. It's a real dilemma."

"Well, I am really in no position to evaluate the gamble. We're talking about my career here. How can it be that my future as a doctor depends upon whether a temporary typist fixed some typos while the form was in the machine—in which case I'm innocent—or rolled the paper out of the machine and rolled it back in—in which case it looks like I'm guilty, which I'm not? How can the law be like that?"

"The law allows the lawyers to argue any inference that the facts support, and here the facts could support both a sinister *and* an innocent inference. How confidently we handle the erasures in front of the jury may well be our best argument as to the innocence of the erasures. What do you want to do?"

"It looks to me like any decision that's made here has downsides. Since you're the one who's got to implement whatever decision is made, you're in the best position to make it. You decide. Don't screw it up," the doctor said grimly and abruptly walked away.

During the afternoon and early evening, my associate arranged meetings later in the evening with questioned document examiners we could potentially call as witnesses. I used that time to telephone my closest lawyer friends to ask them whether they had any additional thoughts about how to handle this decision. They did not and wished me luck. I interviewed the questioned document examiner prospects and selected one to use the next day if we decided to go in that direction.

At 9:00 p.m. that evening, I sat alone in my hotel room, knowing that I had until 9:00 a.m. the next day to decide what to do. I lined out a sheet of paper with "pros" and "cons" and listed all of the options and considerations I could think of. After an hour or two of studying the sheet of paper, I formulated exactly what the essence of the issue for me was: Do I hire a questioned documents examiner or not?

Suddenly, as a "knowing" and not as a guess or a logically arrived-at conclusion, the words came offhandedly into my mind: "Don't worry. It's just typos. Hire the examiner." I remember the words because I wrote them down on the "pros" and "cons" sheet as soon as they floated into my mind. I felt a certain peace after the words came into my mind, and the decision was made.

The next morning, the judge supervised the examination of the original forms in question by the three questioned documents examiners (one hired by each of the three sides remaining in the case). The plaintiffs' examiner went first and studied the forms, placing his grid over the documents and studying the "Wite-Out" portions of the documents carefully.

"Can you tell anything from looking at the documents?" the judge asked the plaintiffs' examiner.

"Well, when I put the grid on the documents, I can't really detect much variation in the horizontal and vertical spacing of the original typed letters as compared to the letters typed over whatever has been Wited-Out. All of the letters typed on the page are pretty much in alignment with each other."

"Can you tell anything about the documents from the fact that you can't detect very much variation in the alignment?"

The plaintiffs' examiner paused for a moment, looked at the forms again, and said: "Yes. Because it is very difficult to reinsert a document into a typewriter carriage and to realign the vertical and horizontal spacing accurately, I would say that the original typing, the erasures, the Wite-Out, and the subsequent typing were all applied while the sheets of paper were still in their original position in the typewriter. I would have to think that the most likely explanation from the appearance of the documents is that it's just typos corrected by the secretary while filling out the forms still in their original position in the typewriter."

"YES!" my heart sang out beneath my poker-face exterior.

Later, the plaintiffs' expert gave similar testimony to the jury. No one cross-examined the plaintiffs' document expert, and there was no need to call our expert. The jury returned a verdict in favor of the doctor and the insurance company, and the plaintiff went away somewhat appeased with the settlement he had made with his employer on the first day of trial.

A few years later, I ran into the doctor at a party at a mutual friend's home. We said hello and chatted for a few minutes. Then the doctor said, "I've thought a lot about the risk we took in handling that document examination, and I often wondered how sure you were that things were going to work out all right before the examiners actually looked at the documents. Was it just a lucky break?"

I laughed and said, "You may find it a little bit strange, but there was no doubt in my mind that the examination was going to come out our way. There was nothing logical about the decision; I just 'knew' it was right. Funny thing is that I have incorporated the procedure I stumbled on in your case in my other cases when a dilemma pops up."

"How so?"

"Well, whenever I want the benefit of intuition, I formulate a question that to me epitomizes my dilemma. I take a moment to quiet my mind, ask my question, expect to get an answer, and write down anything that comes. Many times no intuition comes, and I 'logic' the problem out. But whenever intuition *does* come—and I mean a real 'knowing' and not just a guess—I follow it. So far, my intuition has yet to steer me wrong."

"Did you learn anything else from my case?"

"Yes, tell all of my doctor clients to fill out their patient cards using a computer, not a carriage typewriter."

CHAPTER SEVEN

IT'S IN THE CARDS

"Prophecy is a good line of business, but it is full of risks." —Mark Twain

"You learn how to do what you do well, and then, that's what you do," said my wife, Annie.

"But there must be something else," I persisted. We were sitting in the breakfast nook in our kitchen, overlooking the Pacific, having coffee and enjoying the serenity of the ocean on a calm day. The way the conversation was going, though, indicated that our serenity was quickly dissolving.

"I've got a good law firm partnership," I continued, "enough income, and future prospects; but I don't feel like it's really *helping* anything. I feel like I've worked hard for twenty years just to get myself into a position to work hard for *another* twenty years."

"I don't know what to tell you. You've got pretty much everything you've wanted. You're a lawyer. Be that and just enjoy it."

"But I'm *not* enjoying it. That's the problem! I just see an endless string of 14-hour work days stretching out into the future; *but I can't think of anything else to do.*"

Annie and I had had this conversation before. I had accomplished the goals I had set for myself *years* ago, but now what? It felt useless just to keep grinding away on a dream that had already been achieved.

"Why not take a vacation? You'll feel better."

"Until I go back to work and the feeling of the vacation is gone in a week," I complained. "If there was something else I felt really drawn to, I would do it; but nothing really excites me. So I just keep doing what I'm doing, and keep feeling dissatisfied about it."

Annie smiled and turned away. We both knew that the quest for a meaningful life was personal and that no one could tell me exactly how to find significance in my life.

"Maybe I should try something New Age," I said, not knowing what that meant exactly. "Maybe that can show me how to figure out what to do."

"Sure, why not," she said, getting a little exasperated with this increasingly frequent, solution-less conversation.

"Okay, let's do it," I said. "Let's go to a New Age bookstore and see if there's anything there that looks interesting."

We got in the car and drove to a nearby bookstore. Stepping into the store, I asked the clerk behind the counter, "Can you tell me what to read so that I can learn something about the New Age?"

"What do you mean?" the clerk asked. "There's *so* much different territory there that I couldn't *begin* to describe it to you," she said.

"Thank you," I said, as I began to leave the store, frustrated by the clerk's unwillingness to help at all. On the way back to the car, we passed a storefront that had a sign, "Psychic Fair Today. $5 for 15-Minute Reading."

I looked at Annie, laughed, and said, "Let's go straight to the source and skip this looking in books first."

She seemed skeptical but agreed to come inside with me.

I had never thought much about psychic phenomena, but I was always curious and occasionally saw surprising demonstrations of the power of the mind. Once, for example, I was trying a case for a client who was a strong believer in psychics. While we were picking the jury for the client's case, the client was consulting a psychic about the jurors being selected by the lawyers in the *voir dire* process (the questioning of potential jurors for bias). Near the end of jury selection, when we had one remaining peremptory challenge (which is the right to exclude a potential juror without having to show bias), the client asked us to challenge two jurors. His psychic had said that the rest of the jury would vote for us but that those two prospective jurors would vote against us. I always believed that the client's preference was important in jury selection; and, anyway, I felt that there were more favorable potential jurors in the remaining jury pool than the two jurors in question. Consequently, we used our last peremptory challenge on one of the requested jurors and not the other. The potential juror on the exercised challenge was excused, and the other prospective juror ended up being the only juror who voted against us in an 11-1 verdict. Because a unanimous verdict was not required in that case, we won the trial; but the psychic's accurate prediction (at least twelve out of twelve; the eleven who voted for us and the one who voted against us) got my attention and left me open to the possibilities.

Inside the store, there were four or five little tables, each with a reader and a deck of tarot cards. We had apparently arrived just as the store had opened, and none of the readers was busy. As I looked around, one of the readers—petite and about my age—seemed right, and I sat down at her table. Her name was Isabel, and as we chatted for a few moments, she revealed that she had gone to the same university back east that I had attended—a good sign.

"This is my first psychic fair," Isabel said, laughing. "I thought I'd try it to see whether I got any new business."

"Mine too," I said, already a bit amused myself.

She explained her approach to tarot, had me shuffle and cut the cards, laid out ten of them in a pattern, and began to talk about the cards. One card in an important position was the Four of Pentacles, which is a picture of a princely figure greedily clutching four large coins, or pentacles.

Isabel said that the card represented an aspect of me, that I had achieved a great deal in business, but that holding onto my present position might not be the best thing for me. She added that I might be resisting the flow of change in my life to my detriment.

"As you can see," she said, "the figure is holding very hard onto something that's quite valuable but ultimately not worth the cost."

You got that right, I thought to myself. I was intrigued by the quick reading and asked for a business card for an appointment for a full-length session.

A few weeks later, I met Isabel at the office she'd set up in her home to give tarot readings to regular clients. As we sat across from each other, she laid out on the low table between us a "spread" of twelve cards. She explained the meanings of many of the cards, the reasons for the layout of the cards in patterns, and what various overall patterns meant. She also explained that the images on the cards often triggered intuitive insights in her mind and that her insights, which took into account what she knew about the person before her, were often as valuable as a recitation of the general meaning of the cards themselves.

"Do you have any questions before we begin?"

"Yes. Will I meet my business goals, and will I win the case I'm currently trying?" I asked. At the time, I was engaged in the trial of a very difficult case, and I was also working on greatly expanding my business.

"Let's see what the cards say."

She laid out another spread and exclaimed, "Yes, you will meet your business goals." She pondered the cards further and then said, "I don't say you will lose the case you are trying, but it is difficult, and unexpected things will happen with your witnesses."

She moved on and made several more comments about my business and personal life. When she got to one of the cards in the spread with an obvious spiritual theme, she casually asked, "How do you pray?"

Without thinking about it, I blurted out, "I don't know how to pray."

And, in pondering my spontaneous answer later, I realized that it was true. I had attended religious schools as a child and had learned a great deal of individual prayers, Bible history, and religious ritual; but I did not feel that reciting memorized paragraphs or participating in religious rituals had really ever done much for me spiritually. To me, prayer should somehow be a personal connection with the divine or the eternal, in a way that made daily life meaningful in a sacred or spiritual sense. It did not seem to me that the prayers and rituals I had learned as a child did that. So, I had been accurate in what I'd blurted out. I didn't know how to pray because I didn't know how to make prayer personal. In any event, my own answer shocked and surprised me.

Isabel just laughed and continued to lay out more cards. One of the cards was titled "The Hermit." It depicts an old man with a scholar's cap, leaning on a staff, and holding up a lighted lantern into the night.

She laughed again and said, "Your teacher is coming."

"What does that mean?"

"There's an old Buddhist proverb that says, 'When the student is ready, the teacher will appear,'" she said, "and The Hermit is the card for the entry into your life of a wise guide or spiritual mentor. I say again, your teacher is coming."

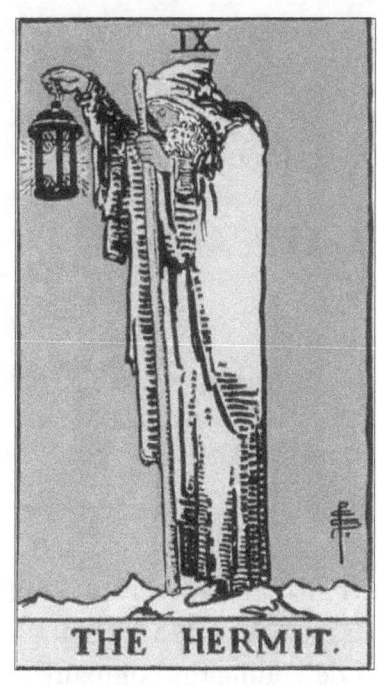

"Who? When?"

"The cards do not say, but you will know it when it happens."

She went on with the reading (which again included the miserly Four of Pentacles) and finished with some general advice about the tarot.

"I'm pretty accurate, or so my clients tell me. But I tell them to use me sparingly—don't come to me for every little decision in life and don't slavishly follow what I see in the cards. Trying to follow the tarot is like what Shakespeare showed about prophecy in Macbeth: much prophecy comes true but never in the way that you expect. So have a tarot reading once a year or so, for comfort, maybe even general guidance; but don't get hooked on it. The universe respects and demands free will."

She finished the reading, and we went our separate ways. After that experience, I didn't know what to believe about tarot readings; but I do know that my first witness in the difficult trial unexpectedly began to volunteer his personal conclusions about the company's problems, effectively losing the case for us on the first day of a six-week trial. And I do know that I tripled my business. After that, I was on the lookout for a teacher.

CHAPTER EIGHT

THE TEACHER APPEARS

"The teacher who is indeed wise does not bid you to enter the house of his wisdom, but rather leads you to the threshold of your mind."—*Kahlil Gibran*

A FEW MONTHS AFTER THE TAROT READING, I received a call from the Syracuse-based general counsel of a Pittsburgh specialty steel company about defending the company in a case involving one of their products. A major oil company had installed the small company's stainless steel tubes in one of its huge heat exchangers used to cool oil down during various stages of the hydrocracking process that produced gasoline in their Los Angeles plant. Somehow, the tubes were either too weak or had somehow gotten infused with hydrogen atoms that wedged themselves between the iron atoms—like sand in a gear—thus making the tubes brittle. When the force of the hydrocracking process was applied, the tubes cracked and leaked partially-refined oil, which led to a refinery explosion that destroyed the heat exchanger and surrounding equipment. Fortunately, no one was injured; but the property damage was a seven-figure number. I agreed to take the matter on, and the general counsel said that he would send out a representative from the company to brief me on the matter. We arranged to meet for breakfast near a local hotel.

"Hello, my name is Walter," said a tall man who approached me just as I arrived at the appointed time and place. About as old as my father, Walter spoke in a deep, slow voice. He seemed friendly but guarded. Regardless, I liked the coincidence that he had the same name as my favorite uncle Walter, who had died a few years earlier. We talked about the case, and he outlined the science of the dispute to me. When I asked how he knew so much about the problem, Walter explained that he was a metallurgical engineer who had worked for this company for many years. He had, in fact, been its chief technology officer when he was working full-time.

"After I retired ten years ago," he said, "the company asked me to help out on a part-time basis with any products liability cases they were involved in."

Walter knew the technology intimately, knew all of the key company personnel in its four or five plant locations, and knew the company's document procedures; so he could be extremely helpful to outside counsel (and the company's general counsel) during document discovery and the overall handling of the case.

We ordered breakfast, and I noticed that Walter ordered only fruit.

"Wouldn't you like something more substantial to go with that?" I asked. "This restaurant is famous for its beef and ham."

"I don't eat meat."

"Oh, why not?"

"Because I'm a vegetarian."

Chancing to push it a little further, even though this was a first meeting, I asked, "Is that for spiritual or health reasons?"

"Both," Walter said, in a way that signaled the end of this line of conversation.

I dropped the subject and returned to discussing the case. Over the course of the next few hours, I came to appreciate that this man was a careful scientist, very intelligent, and possessed of an excellent grasp of the legal principles involved in this type of case. In my experience, it was quite rare for someone with a science mind, focused principally on that which can be verified experimentally, *also* to have a facility for the nebulous art of shaping the application of general principles of law to specific facts in resolving an actual case. That is, in science, it's black or white; in law, it's all gray. But Walter was comfortable in both ways of thinking. He was also no fool, having been the manager of dozens of industrial scientists and the coordinator of thousands of steel contracts during the decades of his work for his company. Yet, he continued to be guarded—polite, helpful, and open regarding the case we were working on—but also a bit impersonal, as though he were sizing me up. We finished our work that day, and I drove Walter to the airport for his flight home, arranging to meet again a few weeks later in Pittsburgh, where the company's technical facilities were located.

In Pittsburgh, we interviewed the company's technical experts together and collected the company's documents relevant to the case. I had planned to stay an extra day to complete my document review, but Walter was flying home a day early, although his flight was not until late in the evening. I suggested that we have dinner before his flight, and Walter agreed. After we finished going over the details of the case at dinner, I was curious about the vegetarian remark Walter had made at our first breakfast meeting in Los Angeles; and, because we had gotten to know each other a little better since our first meeting, I decided to ask him about it.

"When we first got together in Los Angeles, you mentioned that you were a vegetarian," I said. "How did you get started on that?"

"Oh, I was always a big meat eater, but when I was in my late fifties, I got interested in spiritual matters. I began to study with a few spiritual teachers and finally settled on one who taught that the vibrations we get from ingesting meat interfere with our spiritual connection. I tried eating vegetarian for awhile, and it agreed with me: I got fewer colds and flu, I felt better, and I found that I could meditate more easily if I didn't eat meat. So, after that, it just became a habit."

"So you would recommend it then?"

"Well, I really don't recommend anything. Each person is on their own path, which they must take at their own pace. I've known spiritual teachers, for example, who enjoyed a good steak; they said they would just transmute the energy into something positive." He laughed. "But I don't talk about spiritual subjects unless people ask."

"Why is that?"

"Because the only time real spiritual learning takes place is when people are ready to listen; and the best way to tell whether people are ready to listen is when they ask you about it."

Because Walter had talked about his spirituality so openly, I thought I would risk a bold question. "Do you have a religious preference?"

Walter took it in stride. "Not really. All of the world's great religions teach essentially the same things. I am a Christian, but I recognize that the same spiritual truths have been transmitted to believers in all religions."

Emboldened, I tried another risky question. "You mentioned meditation. How did you get into meditation?"

Again, Walter fielded my question effortlessly, as if he felt he could now trust me with meaningful answers. "One of the first spiritual teachers I started working with, in my late fifties, recommended meditation. I tried it, and again, it agreed with me; so I kept up the practice."

I was getting interested now. "If I may, how did meditation agree with you?"

Walter never hesitated in answering honestly. "Well, in my job as an overall manager in the company, I was subject to a lot of pressure and a lot of responsibility when things went wrong. So, I found myself getting mad a lot: getting mad at employees who didn't do their jobs, mad at customers with unrealistic expectations, mad at family members for various reasons, mad at everyone. I would have two or three martinis at the end of each work day, just to forget about the things that I had gotten mad about during the day. When I started meditating, all of that just went away. I found I was more compassionate with those I worked with, more understanding of the circumstances of life, and more forgiving of myself. The funny thing is that I became more effective at what I did—not less effective—than I was when I was angry all of the time. Meditation allowed me to center in myself and on what was really important."

"I never learned how to meditate," I said. "I would like to try it sometime. How do you do it?"

"Oh, it's as easy as falling asleep, which you do every day. You just have to learn how to quiet your mind and still stay awake; but that's easy too. Just pick a practice that suits you."

"There are different ways to meditate?"

"There are probably as many different ways to meditate as there are religions and cultures in the world—some involve emptying the mind of all thoughts; some focus on breathing or on a phrase or mantra to achieve a quiet mind; some instruct you to simply witness everything that's going on without thinking about it. There are dozens of books and courses on different ways to meditate, and any one of them can get you started."

"If I may, what works best for you?"

"I mentally go through a series of steps to get to a quiet place, to invite the Inner Voice. I then ask whatever question is troubling me at the moment and wait for an answer, which often comes. I then follow whatever direction I get."

"Very, very interesting. If you don't mind, Walter, can I ask you if there's anything else I should know before I give meditating a try?"

"Yes. When you go down this road, strange things will start to happen."

"Strange things? What kind of strange things?"

"I don't know specifically what will happen in any particular case, but you will see."

It felt good having a meaningful conversation instead of the usual work talk and chit chat. Walter and I finished dinner, said goodbye, and went our separate ways.

The next morning I got up to complete the remaining document review tasks that I wanted to accomplish on this particular trip. I got dressed, packed my bag to leave for the airport directly from the client's offices, and pressed the elevator "Down" button. The elevator arrived full of people, and I got on. At the lobby, I stepped aside to let a group of women off.

When nearly everyone had gotten off, I heard from the back of the elevator, "Hello, Jim."

I turned around to see standing there, smiling, an old Los Angeles client whom I had not spoken to in at least ten years. Funny thing was, this client now lived outside of Boston, I lived in Los Angeles, and here we were on the same elevator at the same time in Pittsburgh! *What were the chances of that happening?* I wondered. The client had become a famous author of diet books and was in Pittsburgh to attend a convention on diet supplements for athletes, and I was on my way out of Pittsburgh after a document review for a client. But to be on the same elevator at exactly the same time?

Way beyond coincidence, I thought to myself.

I chatted with the author for a few moments, and we renewed our friendship. Later, we did some more legal work together and continued to stay in touch—all from a chance meeting in an elevator in a city that neither of us frequented. That got my attention; and with Walter's statement, "Strange things will start to happen" ringing in my mind, I determined to study this all further.

When I got some free time in Los Angeles, I went

to a New Age bookstore, looking for something on the powers of the mind. I surveyed several books, but they all seemed too far out. Finally, I came upon a series of simply written books about the Silva Mind Control program. I looked at the details of their approach and decided to take one of the Silva courses offered in Los Angeles. When I did, I quickly realized that the course, in a slow, methodical, and complete way, was teaching, essentially, how to meditate or "go to the theta brain wave level," as they put it. The course went on to teach the affirmative use of intuition, how to use meditation and intuition to solve everyday problems, and how to get answers to your most pressing, personal questions. I was fascinated that I had stumbled upon something so practical.

After I'd had the incredible experience of dreaming about Sonny's death before it happened, while taking the Silva course, I decided to try the techniques taught in the course. Rather quickly, I began to get helpful answers to questions that had puzzled me for some time. But I also was skeptical—how could quieting my mind, asking a question, waiting for an answer, and then acting on the answer (when I felt I had received a real "knowing," as opposed to simply a guess) apply to "real world" situations? I kept playing with it.

Finally, I tried it out on something substantial, something "real." Pre-trial proceedings in Walter's case were pending before the court and included a series of motions we had made to get the court to order the other side to produce certain items of discovery for our inspection. Such motions were expensive to make and were effectively non-appealable; we needed the missing items immediately in order to prepare our defense; and if we did not get what we were asking for, we might never be able to develop the evidence necessary to defend the case; so a lot was riding on the outcome of these motions.

In this particular court, there was only one judge assigned to handle motions of this type, and there were literally hundreds of complicated motions in many different cases pending before him at any one time. In order to get the motions resolved *and* to keep the cases moving toward trial, the judge would assign each of the motions to one of his many court commissioners, who would review the motion paperwork and prepare a tentative decision. If the parties agreed to stipulate on the day of the hearing to have the commissioner decide the motion—and to waive their right to a decision by a duly-elected Superior Court judge—the commissioner could render a decision on the day of the hearing. If there was no stipulation, the matter would be referred for decision back to the judge, who because of his workload, could take *months* to decide any particular motion—too long a delay for our case. *And* there was no guarantee that the judge would eventually decide the motions in our favor. The parties were not told until the day of the hearing what the commissioner's tentative decision was on their motions. Before the hearing on the motions, the junior partner handling this aspect of the case and I had gone over the commissioners' records and had decided that the commissioner assigned to our case was unlikely to be favorable to our type of motion.

When the day of the hearing arrived, the junior partner called from the court house. "I know that we have decided that the commissioner assigned to our case is not good for us, but the tentative ruling is in our favor," he said.

"What's the tentative ruling?"

"It just says 'Grant' next to our motions on the calendar; so we don't know whether the assigned commissioner will give us a little bit of what we're asking for, or a lot, or nothing at all, after the commissioner hears argument from both sides. Should I stipulate to the commissioner or kick it back to the judge?"

"What did the other side do?"

"Because they knew who the commissioner was, they stipulated right away and waived their right to have the judge decide. So we can have a decision today, but we really don't know what the commissioner will end up deciding until after the argument is over; and we won't know what the judge will decide to do in a couple of months when he finally gets around to our motion if we don't stipulate to the commissioner today."

"How much time do we have?"

"I told the clerk that I needed to make a phone call; so everyone's basically waiting on us."

"What do you think?" I asked.

"Normally, I'd say call the client to make the decision; but we don't have time to explain all of the considerations, if we ever could. It's really up to you."

I took a deep breath. There was no logical indication of how any decision here might turn out. The commissioner's tentative decision had been "Grant," but many tentative decisions end up going the other way after argument; and maybe "grant" was typed in erroneously by a clerk, instead of "deny," as the commissioner may have intended.

If there was ever a time to see whether what I had learned in the Silva course about the active use of intuition *really* worked, this was the time to do it. I decided to give it a shot.

I stated the question mentally, "Do we stipulate to the commissioner?" and waited for an answer. Almost immediately, I got the strong feeling: "Stipulate to the commissioner."

I took another deep breath and told the junior partner, "Make the stipulation to the commissioner and good luck with the argument."

"OK," he replied. "I'll call you as soon as it's over."

It was a tense three hours before I got his call back.

"Long argument," he said, "and the commissioner went overboard, *in our favor*."

After that, I started to believe in meditation.

The commissioner's ruling ultimately resulted in the other side's production of thousands of pages of technical documents that required review by a scientist, so Walter volunteered to come out to Los Angeles to do the job. He reviewed documents in our offices for several days. When Friday arrived, I asked him when he was flying home.

"I'm not finished reviewing the documents, so I thought I would take the weekend to complete the job."

"OK. I admire your tenacity, but reviewing documents is no way to spend a Friday night. Tonight, my wife and I are going out with some friends to see a modern art exhibit that just opened in downtown Los Angeles. Why don't you come with us, and we'll all go out to dinner afterwards?"

"Sure, sounds great."

We had an enjoyable Friday evening, and Annie, also a vegetarian, invited Walter out to visit the house and have Saturday night dinner with us at a local vegetarian restaurant. After Saturday's dinner, we started asking Walter some questions about how he became interested in spirituality.

"Well, my wife was seeing a spiritual advisor in Ohio, and she asked me to go along with her to a meeting. I did and I enjoyed it, so I kept going. That advisor died, and we found our current advisor about ten years ago."

"Is this like a guru?" I asked.

"Heavens, no. I'm a scientist, and I accept nothing unless I believe it's absolutely correct. Anything this spiritual advisor says I verify with my own inner voice. If my inner voice agrees, I accept what the advisor says; if not, I go my own way. To her credit, our advisor also insists that each of her students accept only what resonates with them and reject whatever else she says that doesn't feel true."

"How does your spiritual advisor do her teaching?"

"We get together at her place in rural Virginia or other places she feels drawn to work with us. We talk about the subjects we're learning and meditate together, and she guides us about the subjects."

"What subjects does your advisor teach? Do you just go over the Bible?"

"No, I believe the Bible is important, and I have studied it on my own and through my church for many years," Walter said. "But it was written two thousand years ago; and there is much, much more to be known about the universe than the Bible revealed at an earlier time in human development."

"Where does the additional information come from? From 'channeling'?"

"No, our spiritual advisor is something of a mystic; but she finds *The Urantia Book* to be an excellent source of what she feels to be accurate information about how the universe works."

"What's *The Urantia Book*? I've never heard of it."

"It's a spiritual book that originated in Chicago in the 1920s and 1930s. It's over 2,000 pages long and is divided into 196 essays, or "papers," said to have been authored by a variety of the universe's celestial entities. The papers discuss God, science, life and death, personality survival, the structure of the universe, the universe's various spiritual entities, and the history of the earth, which is called 'Urantia' everywhere else in the universe."

"How's it different from the Bible?"

Walter shook his head and declared that he didn't find the two books to be all that different. "*The Urantia Book* just expands upon what's in the Bible and adds concepts that aren't mentioned in the Bible. In fact, there's a thick book that you can buy, called a *Concordex*, that compares what's in *The Urantia Book* to similar passages in the Bible covering the same subjects. There's no essential conflict between the two books; *The Urantia Book* just has additional information. For example, the Old Testament in the Bible mentions the Ancient of Days but doesn't really elaborate on the function of this type of celestial being. *The Urantia Book* discusses the Ancients of Days in some detail, outlines their universe duties and responsibilities, and describes how they fit into the overall system of universe administration."

"Who wrote the book?"

"The book itself describes how a group of humans got the information through a human subject whose 'divinity within' transmitted the words of each paper from the celestial being who authored it. The group recorded the information, collected it into a book, and began publishing the book in the mid-1950s."

"How can you tell whether the book is credible?"

"To me, it's kind of self-authenticating. The book has many original, profound passages; it is very well written, and the writing style of each 'paper' is different. It is highly internally consistent. Also, the Urantia Foundation that originally published the book never advocated the formation of a church to honor the book. It's interesting—the Urantia Foundation is a tiny organization that's actually in the process of losing the copyright to the book. Since they maintain that it was not written by humans, but by celestial beings, and since the courts don't recognize celestial beings as copyright holders, they don't stand a good chance of holding onto the copyright. This low-key stance by the Foundation gives the book even *more* credibility, in my mind. They don't have any ax to grind; they're not trying to build any empires, like many religions do. They're just trying to do what they think is right by getting the word out. Even if the book were only science fiction, I think it's worth reading because its main themes are ones I believe in: friendliness, non-violence, and service to others.

"Can the book be purchased?"

"Sure, you can find it at most bookstores."

"Curious. Incidentally, Walter, I noticed that you're not having anything to drink. Do you mind my asking why that is?"

"Oh, I stopped drinking a couple of years ago."

"Why did you stop?"

"Well, I used to really enjoy drinks after work; but I was meditating one day after having had far too many drinks. When I tried to get my mind back to the everyday waking state, I couldn't find my way. That scared me a little. Also, I found that drinking interfered with my connection with Spirit, which was more important to me than drinking."

"How did you stop?" I asked. As with every trial lawyer I ever knew, drinking went with the territory, and I was always curious about how people were able to give it up.

Walter just smiled and said, "Start meditating regularly, and you'll see what happens."

I laughed, and we went on to enjoy the rest of the evening. Walter finished up his work and flew back home the next day. We continued to work together on the case and began to get together in Los Angeles every few weeks. During Walter's next visit, we had dinner together every night, and when work was through, I continued to pepper him with questions about spiritual matters. Walter always obliged me with thoughtful, helpful answers.

Our next meeting was arranged for me to travel to the company's Wisconsin plant in January, in order to meet with Walter and other company executives, including its general counsel. This location is where the products involved in the case had actually been manufactured. The flights from Los Angeles to Wisconsin entailed several plane changes, followed by an hour's drive from the airport in Milwaukee to the plant site. The weather was bad, and the flights were bumpy. I knew that when I arrived I would be subjected to a particularly difficult dinner meeting format, one typically favored by the general counsel: following the long trip and after several rounds of dinner drinks, I would be cross-examined on where the case was going, what it was going to cost, and how I was going to solve the company's case problems. I was *not* looking forward to the dinner, and I had a blinding headache by the time I arrived. But I made the best of it and got through the experience, while reassuring the company that the case was moving in the right direction.

Before we started interviewing witnesses the next morning, Walter pulled me aside and said, "I'm delighted to see that you've decided to go down the spiritual path. That's great! There's no turning back, though."

"How do you know that I've decided to go down the spiritual path?"

"I saw it in your aura when you walked into the restaurant for the dinner meeting last night."

Marveling that anyone could have seen anything about me through the fog of last night's headache, I said: "You never told me that you could see auras."

Walter laughed and said, "You never asked."

The Silva course had a segment on using the mind to see auras, and even I could do it occasionally when the person in front of me was very upset, or angry, or completely relaxed and thinking about something they loved. I wasn't very good at it; but I knew that it could be done, that some people (like medieval artists who painted saints with halos) were *quite* good at it, and that still others had had the ability to see auras ever since they were children.

And I guess it was true (i.e., Walter was right) about my venturing onto a spiritual path. I had been trying out meditating; I had had the experience of following my intuition in stipulating to the commissioner; and I *had* made the conscious decision to let the spiritual path take me wherever it wanted to go, at least for a while.

Following that decision, another thing had started to happen: I was drinking less and less, finding that even one glass of a good Chianti with dinner would leave me with a hangover the next morning. So I had virtually stopped drinking (except on business occasions, such as at the previous night's dinner meeting) because it physically hurt more than it helped, which surprised me.

I told Walter about my recent experience with not drinking, and he said, "I wouldn't be surprised if Spirit has you take a break from drinking for a few years."

"Why do you think that?"

Walter just laughed and said, "Well, we'll see what happens." (Indeed, I ended up not drinking alcohol for the next five years.)

We finished up our work in Wisconsin and started discussing our next meeting in Los Angeles. Suddenly, it popped into my mind, and I found myself saying, "Why don't you stay at my house the next time you come out, instead of getting a hotel room? We have plenty of space, now that my son is in college, and we enjoy the conversation."

"I'd like that," Walter said.

On his next visit, he handed me a package when I picked him up at the airport.

"What's this?"

"A present from me to you. Your own copy of *The Urantia Book*."

"When am I ever going to read that? Isn't my school learning over?"

"Like *The Urantia Book* says, the universe is one vast school for evolving mortals and learning can take all eternity." Walter smiled. "So, you've got time."

I laughed, said thanks, and put it on the back seat. But when Walter finished his work and went back home, I found the time and began reading. At first, it was very slow going. I could read, at most, only a paragraph at a time before I began to fall asleep. This was not because the book was boring—it's actually very exciting—but because it was so dense. Like a play that starts in the middle of a story without introducing any of its characters, *The Urantia Book* begins by narrating about dozens of new characters, events, and principles, *none* of which I had ever heard of before; *plus* some familiar characters cast in entirely new lights, like Adam and Eve, Lucifer, and Abraham. Reading the Bible and *The Urantia Book* was like reading a description of the same events by two different participants in those events, one human and one celestial: they're both describing exactly the same events but from totally different perspectives.

Slowly, the structure of the universe and the cosmology of the earth the book portrayed began to make sense, and I could read the book like any other. But reading a page or two at a time was the limit of what I could ever absorb before having to stop. What did I conclude about the book? I don't know where it came from or whether it was authentic; but it was certainly profound in an astonishing variety of areas, law being just one of many. (For example, "The argumentative defense of any proposition is inversely proportional to the truth contained," and, "[T]he status of any civilization may be very accurately determined by the thoroughness and equity of its courts and by the integrity of its judges.") Regardless of its source or whether its authors were celestial spirits, the book made sense to me, sense worth paying attention to.

For the next two years, Walter and I followed a pattern in working together on the case: he would come to Los Angeles to work and would stay at my home. We would work hard on the case during the day but would spend our free time together talking about spiritual matters. We both enjoyed the exchange. The two of us worked up a terrific defense for the case, and I learned a lot about spiritual matters.

So much so, that I once asked Walter, "I'm sort of curious, Walter. Why do you take all of the time and care that you do to go over these spiritual matters with me?"

"Well, I think the universe is like a big ladder: the person on the rung above you reaches down to give you a hand up; and, in turn, you reach your hand down to the person on the next lower rung to give them a hand up. Besides, I feel honored to have been the one selected by the universe to answer your questions, and I want to take great care and meditation time to make sure that I'm getting it right."

"Thank you for that. And if you're willing, I'll keep asking."

Walter laughed and said, "Ask away."

"Actually, there is something I've been having difficulty with. Many times in meditation, I ask a question like 'What should I be doing with my life?' and I don't get an answer. I wonder why not."

"Try asking focused 'yes' or 'no' questions instead of open-ended questions. And remember that the future might not yet be set as to the subject of your question; so the answer might not yet be available. But keep at it, and you'll get some direction at some point, when the time is right. Sometimes, a spiritual teacher can help out when you get stuck."

"How does your spiritual teacher help you get unstuck?"

"I think I might have mentioned before that my wife and I get together with the teacher and five or six of her other students every couple of months for guided meditations. That helps because the group meditation generates a special energy—not usually available when one meditates alone—that seems to facilitate understanding. Also, the teacher will prepare an alignment chart for any of her students desiring one. You can ask any questions; the teacher will meditate on them; and in a 10- or 12-page presentation suggest answers or ways to find the answers, as well as other areas you might want to look at in your life."

"Who are the other students?"

"Just people who have come in contact with Crystal in one way or another over the years. By profession, there's a school teacher or two, a non-practicing lawyer, an engineer (me), some stay-at-home moms, and several others. One of the teachers is a professor at Germany's equivalent to West Point in Munich; one of the housewives is from Australia; a couple of people are from England; there's a minister's wife from Nigeria; others are from the United States—Virginia, New Mexico, New York, California."

"'Crystal' sounds like the name of a guru."

"Oh, her students wouldn't put up with anything like a guru. Crystal told me once that it was revealed to her in meditation to use that name, instead of her given name of Patricia, so as to help her students get over negative judgments about unimportant things, like what someone's name is. Crystal always insists that her students be guided solely by their own inner voice and not by anything she says just because she said it. She sees herself as a facilitator, not as an organizer. I think that she has a strong connection to Spirit and just wants to share what she gets or what she has with anyone who is interested. The most important thing I can say about who Crystal is is that I have never seen her act or react toward anything in any way *other* than with unconditional love. I really don't know how she does it, because some of her students can be quite exasperating—asking the same question over and over again, for example—but she always responds to every situation with understanding and impersonal love."

"Sounds like a patient person."

"She is. Would you like to meet her? She's having a seminar about an hour's drive north of Los Angeles next month, and we're flying out together. Why don't you come?"

"I've never studied with a spiritual teacher."

Walter laughed and said, "There's always a first time."

"OK, I'm willing to give it a go."

When Walter and Crystal came to Los Angeles, I picked them up at the airport. I knew that Walter had knee pain from injuries he had sustained many years ago while playing football in college; so I always made sure he could sit in the roomy front passenger seat whenever I picked him up at the airport. This time, he climbed into the tight backseat.

"Sit in front, Walter," I said.

"No, thanks. I want you to be able to sit next to Crystal," he said. Such respect from one whom I respected got my attention.

Crystal (Patricia Jepsen) *and* the seminar were just as Walter had said. She felt like a lifelong friend as soon as we met; and even though I only understood about twenty percent of what was said at the seminar, the students were warm and accepting, and the energy of group meditation was undeniable. I continued to study with her after that, understood more of what she was saying, and happily became a "student"—another gift from Walter.

And speaking of lifelong friends, I always thought that real friends, friends you could say anything to without fear of losing them, were only developed when you both were children. With Walter, I began to think differently. As we continued to work the law case, we continued to spend time together talking about spiritual matters and just things that friends talk about: children, delights, disappointments, and the everyday matters of life. During that time, I came to respect him even more. I remember once at one of the seminars there was a general discussion about what to do if one could not understand why something had happened in his or her life.

Walter spoke up, "When I don't get anything in meditation about a situation, I just stop for a while. I know that Spirit will lead me to the answer when the time is right for me to receive it. My job is to be open to the answer when it comes. To stay open, I redouble my efforts and keep asking until I do get an answer." Knowing Walter, I knew that he meant it.

"Do you ever brood about the failures in your life—the times when you made mistakes and had to pay the price?" I once asked Walter.

"Sure, I've had things in my life that I thought were great sins, as well as small things that didn't work because of my mistakes. But when my thoughts turn to such things, I just think to myself: it happened; I did my best to correct the situation; I've learned that lesson, and I don't have to think about it anymore. The thoughts usually then just go away."

I often wondered what Walter, with his strong spiritual beliefs about love and the brotherhood of man, really thought about law, lawyers, and civil litigation in America; so I asked him about it one day.

"I *have* given that some thought and have come to a conclusion. We need the lawyers. Without them, we'd be going at each other with ax handles."

A lot of wisdom from a layman, I thought.

The law case ultimately came up to a trial date. As we worked diligently to defend the case, we were able to demonstrate that the tubes had likely leaked, *not* because they were unsound—they were found to be within specifications—but because they had become embrittled after being flooded with massive doses of free hydrogen carried in the process stream running through the tubes, a possibility that had *not* been disclosed when the tubes were sold *and* that could not have been anticipated. The unexpectedly large quantity of free hydrogen was what had ignited explosively and had caused the damage to the refinery.

When we appeared for the pre-trial conference, the assigned judge told us, "We've calculated that it costs us $10,000 a day to conduct a jury trial in this courthouse; so we try to settle as many cases as we can. Can you tell me what this case is about?"

Over the next five days, including through the weekend, the judge met with us for five hours a day, exploring every aspect of each party's case. He called in the party's insurers and discussed their participation as well. The case settlement finally hit a sticking point, and the negotiations stalled.

On some previous occasions, I had asked Walter to meditate on a problem I was facing to see whether he received any insights on the problem. He would frequently answer, "No, I'm sorry. This is yours to work out. I'm supposed to stay out of this one."

Walter had often said that meditation was not to be used for predicting the future or to solve someone else's problems. That was all "phenomena," which were astral and to be avoided. However, when the case hit a snag in settlement, I asked him to "check in" to see whether we would ultimately be successful in settlement or whether we should start spending money on serious trial preparation even while the settlement discussions were going on.

Walter left for a few minutes. When he came back, he said only, "It hasn't been determined yet."

We continued to negotiate. Finally, one of my partners had the breakthrough thought to ask the judge, who now thoroughly understood the case and all of the parties, to say in front of the insurance carriers what he thought the case should reasonably settle for. The judge thought about it for a moment, roughed out some figures on a piece of paper, and then gave his opinion. The insurance carriers left to call their offices.

"Would you meditate on this and ask again?" I asked Walter.

He smiled and said, "I already have. The case is over."

And so it was, as the case quickly settled to everyone's satisfaction.

For the next several years, Walter and I continued to talk on the telephone several times a month and to get together at Crystal's seminars, which were held at various places around the country. Most of the time, the seminars consisted of me and Walter and five or six women. Women always greatly outnumbered men at the seminars. I once asked Walter what he thought about why there were mostly women at the seminars and why men were not attending.

Walter smiled and said, "They'll come around." We both laughed.

We also continued to talk with each other about our lives, and when Annie and I decided to divorce, Walter was one of the first ones I called. Walter, who had five children and had been married to his wife for more than fifty years, was a strong believer in marriage; but he was an even stronger believer in following one's spiritual path, no matter where it led.

"I knew from meditation that that had happened," Walter said, "I have no judgment about it. You're following your path."

All disapproval dispelled in a single breath.

A few years later, Crystal moved to Mount Shasta and was holding a seminar there. I had left the full-time practice of law, was living in rural coastal California, and had stopped attending Crystal's seminars, although I stayed in touch with her by telephone and e-mail.

She called one day and said, "Walter and his wife are coming to the seminar. Why don't you bring Lauren and surprise him. I won't say anything about your coming."

That struck me as a splendid idea, so we made the arrangements. I also thought about how to show Walter what he had meant to me in introducing me to the spiritual path. We lived in wine country, where there were several excellent local artists who could etch wine bottles in color. I found one, gave her a glass brick and "The Hermit" tarot card, and asked her to reproduce the image exactly on the glass brick with an inscription. She executed it perfectly, and we packed the brick in our bags for the trip to Mount Shasta.

We did not attend the seminar but timed it so that we would arrive just as the seminar was concluding. I remember driving up to Crystal's place and seeing Walter and his wife sitting on the front porch. Walter did not have his glasses on but was looking at Mount Shasta (no doubt searching its aura). As we pulled into the driveway, Walter looked, then squinted hard, and then exploded into a huge laugh, a tumble of arms and legs, and a big hug. We laughed hard about the surprise and sat down to a lunch that Crystal had prepared, where we all talked about some of the amazing things that we had experienced together over the years.

As lunch was concluding, I said, "Walter, I have something for you in the car. Could you come out to the porch, so I can give it to you?" Everyone gathered on the porch in full view of Mount Shasta.

I gave Walter the glass brick, explained the meaning of The Hermit tarot card, gave him a hug, and read out loud the inscription on the glass block, which was:

When the student is ready, the teacher will appear.
Many thanks from a grateful student.

We had all spent wonderful hours together, working, meditating, learning, laughing, and enduring the lessons of life; and we all were doing pretty well with keeping our emotions in check while I was presenting the glass brick to Walter that day…right up until the moment when Walter's wife began to cry.

Looking back, I realize I had indeed "manifested" what I had been seeking—a teacher to open up my mind to the vast "something else" that my *ennui* was telling me I had been lacking after I had accomplished my earthly goals.

I stayed in touch with Walter, calling every couple of months. He would always ask, "How are you doing spiritually?" and we would talk about spiritual matters. Walter died a few years later, passing away one day in an instant from a heart attack while going to make himself and his wife a glass of carrot juice. And a citizen of the universe left the people of Urantia that day for his next assignment in the celestial university.

CHAPTER NINE

WE THE PEOPLE

"Love thy neighbor."—*Matthew 22:39*

WHEN I WAS A NEW LAWYER, my corporate law firm regularly gave its young litigators the assignment of working for a month with New York's Legal Aid Society, representing indigent defendants in Manhattan's criminal court. The firm believed that the volunteer work gave young litigators valuable trial experience and taught them some gritty truths.

I was thus representing indigent defendants in the criminal court's arraignment department one morning when the court began to call the solicitation calendar. The door to the holding cells opened to the judge's left, into the courtroom, and fifteen or so young women, picked up somewhere in Manhattan the night before for solicitation of prostitution, were led in and seated at the east side of the courtroom. They sat on a long bench, which was separated by a balustrade from the general audience. The women were within, and quite close to, the area where the prosecution and defense (my team) worked.

The process was simple: each woman's case number and name would be called; the prosecution attorney would state his name; the clerk would read the charges; the woman's private defense lawyer would plead the client guilty to a minor misdemeanor; the judge would find the defendant guilty and assess a $100 fine; and the woman would be released to pay the fine and go back home to get some sleep before the next evening's work. This particular morning, the women were making the most of the experience, chatting quietly and laughing before another day began for them.

"Case Number 705687, People of the State of New York versus Belinda Jones. Counsel, please state your appearances," the clerk called out in a voice loud enough for any private attorney for the defendant in the general audience beyond the balustrade to hear.

The young assistant district attorney stood up, holding the manila case file in his left hand, "Anthony Valentino, Your Honor, for the People."

To which one of the women on the bench, in a voice as loud as the clerk's, spontaneously blurted out: "*We* the people. You the government."

Gritty truth and no oath necessary.

I was telling that story to Walter one day while we waited outside of the judge's chambers to begin a settlement conference in the case involving Walter's company.

Walter laughed. "Speaking of people and governments, some of our friends are thinking of going to the Earth Summit in Rio de Janeiro, and Crystal asked my wife and me if we were going."

"Are you going?"

"We really don't feel inspired to make this trip; but

Crystal's going, along with Marilyn and a few others. I was wondering whether you were going."

"First I've heard of it. What's Crystal going to do there? Or Marilyn?"

"Crystal's the head of a small group called Center for International Cooperation that's chartered as an NGO, or non-governmental organization, by the United Nations. Its purpose is to foster peace in the world and to support the health of the earth's ecology, particularly as seen through the eyes of the earth's indigenous people. The UN conference in Rio de Janeiro is called UNCED—the United Nations Conference on Ecology and Development—and the UN invited its NGOs to observe some of the UNCED public sessions. There's also a parallel Global Forum conference of the NGOs going on at the same time in Rio, and Crystal's giving a Global Forum speech or two and participating in Global Forum panel discussions with some of our Native American friends."

"How does Marilyn fit in?"

"Well, Crystal got the idea at a conference of indigenous people in Australia, called Earth-Walk, to make peace with Mother Earth by making a personal treaty to stop doing things that damaged the earth. As you know, Marilyn runs an accredited online school and is interested in ecology. Marilyn got excited about the Earth Treaty idea and collaborated with Crystal in developing an outline for such an Earth Treaty. Then, through the online school, Marilyn worked out an exercise where her teenagers who wanted to participate could each write about their relationship with the earth and what each could do to take care of the earth. Over the years, Marilyn has collected thousands of these Earth Treaties. Crystal suggested that Marilyn go to Rio as the other authorized representative of the Center for International Cooperation and assist her in presenting the Earth Treaties to the world's indigenous women, who are holding their own parliament there. Marilyn thought it was a great idea and is bringing two of her teenage students along to speak about the Earth Treaties at the Global Forum."

"Why is Crystal presenting the treaties to the indigenous women?"

"Well, mothers, Mother Earth, etc. Native people live closest to the earth and typically feel a sense of responsibility as stewards of the land. Also, indigenous people have a very different system of government than we do, at least among the Mohawks, with whom I'm most familiar. In that tribe, the men are the chiefs, but the women have the power to elect the chiefs. When a man is not doing his job as chief to the satisfaction of the women, they vote him out and elect a new chief. Indigenous people seem to be those most concerned about Mother Earth, and native women have power in their society; so native women are the logical choice to receive the children's Earth Treaties."

"Interesting, but if we don't settle this case, we're not going anywhere."

"Well, you were saying that this case is a year away from trial. So, there'll be time for a side-trip. What do you think?"

"Spend my summer vacation in Rio attending a United Nations conference as an observer? I don't know, Walter...."

"Suit yourself. As I said, my wife and I don't feel inspired to go."

We didn't settle Walter's case that day, and the litigation marched forward. A few weeks later, as I was going through my daily stack of mail, I came across a newsletter from the American Bar Association noting that, as a non-governmental organization, the ABA had observer status and could appoint two representatives to attend the public sessions of the UNCED conference. The piece also said that the UN had designated this conference as one where its 172 member states were to be represented in the final sessions by their heads of state. So, it looked like the United Nations was serious about actually getting something done at this conference.

Suddenly, a strong inspiration came to me: call the ABA up and ask to be appointed as one of the two representatives. So, before I could talk myself out of it, I dialed the ABA headquarters in Chicago and asked for the person charged with making the selection. A secretary answered that extension, and I stated my request.

"He's not available right now, but I should tell you that the ABA has 400,000 members, and we only have two slots—and one of them was filled months ago by the Insurance Section. Actually, the second one was also filled some time ago, but that gentleman just received credentials through the State Department to attend the governmental working sessions; so the second slot just opened up again. We've been thinking of having the International Section give us input on filling that slot. I assume you know that we don't reimburse expenses."

"Yes, I thought that might be the case."

"Are you an ABA Delegate or a Council Member of the International Section?"

"No, but I am a member of the ABA and of the International Section."

"Well, the decision has to be made soon so that we can tell the UN. You could try the Chair of the International Section."

I thanked the secretary and hung up. The Chair of the International Section had recently changed, and I had actually met the new chairperson within the past year. Without thinking about it, I telephoned him and asked to be considered.

"Yes, I do remember you from the luncheon. Sure, we'll keep you in mind."

Oh well, 400,000-to-1 are pretty long odds, and it seemed that much political jockeying had already gone on in the process of allocating the ABA's two slots. I went back to working on the matters I was handling.

About a half hour later, the phone rang and it was the ABA secretary I had spoken with that morning in Chicago.

"The ABA has appointed you as its second representative to UNCED."

"Wow, thanks! That was fast!"

"I thought so too," she said with a laugh, before saying goodbye.

I put the telephone down. *What do I really think about this trip now that I'm going? I've never been to Latin America before; I have no real focus on why I am going, other than to just observe, for the first time, a large United Nations conference; participating in the simultaneous, individual-oriented Global Forum might be interesting; several of my friends are going; I'll probably learn some things about the environment and sustainable development; and being appointed, in the face of the 400,000-to-1 odds against it happening, is too serendipitous to ignore. Bottom line: I don't know what to think about it all, but acting on my intuition to call the ABA is what set me on this journey. So why not let the momentum behind that intuitive "hit" take me wherever it's going?*

A few weeks later, I found myself stepping tentatively off of the airplane at Rio de Janeiro's Galeão International Airport. The movies had not prepared me for Rio's spectacular physical setting of Yosemite-like granite domes, hardwood rainforests, urban beaches, 90° degree autumnal heat, and six million racially diverse Brazilians living packed side-by-side in great wealth or abject poverty—all presided over by the dramatic statue of "Cristo Redentor," Rio's iconic symbol set high atop Corcovado mountain and visible day and night from everywhere in Rio. I was *also* not prepared for Rio's cultural diversity, for sacrifices of rooster and grain set out along the sidewalk as meals for the gods by devout African animists, for packs of pre-teen street children roaming the beaches in search of food, for elaborate colonial restaurants serving lavish portions of barbecued beef...and finally, I was not prepared for the amazing spectrum of human beings interested in the Earth Summit! One film I watched at the Global Forum (with simultaneous translations in seven languages) was attended by North and South Americans, Asians, Africans, Europeans, Pacific Islanders, Russians, and

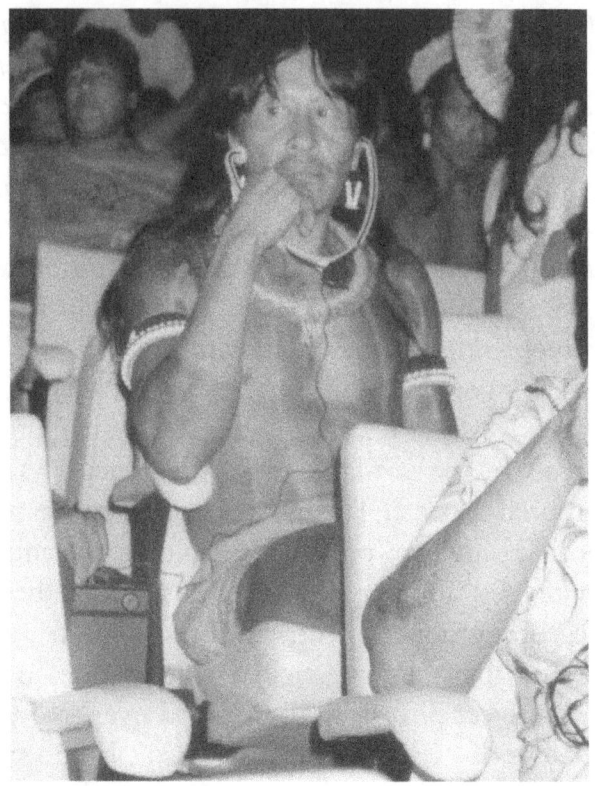

others, all interested, as was the Amazonian above, in what was happening with their Earth.

The Global Forum was held in town and featured exhibits, panel discussions, and speeches by members of the fourteen hundred or so attending NGO organizations, which ran the gamut from environmentally-committed organizations (like the Sierra Club) to professional organizations (like my own American Bar Association) to groups simply representing concerned individual inhabitants of planet Earth (like Crystal's Center for International Cooperation). I attended the Global Forum's informal sessions with tens of thousands of others and was repeatedly jolted by the easy familiarity of remarkable people—Jacques Cousteau, with a hand-held microphone in a large tent, spoke eloquently of his precious sea; the Dalai Lama spoke to several Global Forum audiences; I walked by California's former governor, Jerry Brown, who said hello and asked me how I was doing (I was fine, thank you); Roger Moore (007's on the job), Bella Abzug, and Tom Hayden also spoke.

The event had the same feeling as those I attended in the '60s—and the same people. I attended a speech by an American Senator who was passionate about global warming—Al Gore, just months before he was elected vice president of the United States (and a decade and a half before he won the Nobel Prize). But these people were acting not as governmental officials speaking to their citizens but as regular air-breathing inhabitants of Earth, who had a vision to share with their neighbors about how to protect "the neighborhood."

After the first morning's Global Forum sessions, I happened to be sitting across from Marilyn at lunch.

"Have you had a chance to get down to the beach yet?" I asked.

"Yes, and I loved the gorgeous view of the bay and out into the South Atlantic. I think I saw the descendants of 'The Girl from Ipanema' there too."

We both laughed.

"The beach was spectacular," Marilyn said, "but you have to basically cross a freeway to get to it. There's this wide boulevard between the city and the beach that's always full of noisy trucks spewing exhaust fumes. Talk about ecology!"

"Yes, quite a contrast," I said. "Speaking of ecology, what was it that made you decide to come to Rio for the Earth Summit?"

"Crystal and I talked about the fact that I had collected all of these Earth Treaties from my students over the years and that this was a great opportunity to honor the ecological commitments the students had made by presenting the Treaties here in Rio. I told my former students in person or by e-mail what we're doing, and they're all supportive of the effort. In fact, many of my former students are now working adults, and they contributed financially to the effort so that two current students could come with me—these two, and the others who contributed, will remember this event more vividly than if we took a senior trip to Washington, D.C."

"What will your two seniors do here?"

"They'll each be speaking at two Global Forum events about what the environment means to them. One got interested in the subject because her family lives on a country lane, not far from a landfill. When the landfill is closed or people find out that they have to pay a use fee at the landfill, they sometimes simply dump their trash on the shoulder of her country lane—so she has a personal perspective on how everyone's treatment of the environment affects everyone else."

"How does the young guy fit in?"

"He's very shy, and speaking to a group is quite an accomplishment for him. But he got interested in a movie about aliens. The plot was that aliens had invaded the earth, with a plan to colonize it and wipe out all of the humans. All of Earth's people, including former enemies, had to band together to defeat the aliens. That really struck a chord in him, and he saw the many kinds of ecological damage inflicted upon the earth as being like 'aliens,' which humans had to band together to defeat. That's the talk he developed, and he gives it with lots of feeling, which overcomes his shyness."

"What do the two students do with the rest of their time here?"

"They check out the beach, sightsee in Rio, and talk with the people their age attending the conference from all over the world. They both have plenty to do and are getting an incredible education. Me too!"

Again, we both laughed.

Later that afternoon, Crystal and I, as designated representatives of our respective NGO organizations, traveled to the first session of the official UNCED conference, which was held at the convention center twenty miles outside of town. Military security was everywhere, protecting the world leaders, who were casually wandering around inside, like shareholders at an annual meeting. When we were seated in the NGO section, Daniel Arap Moi, Kenya's long-time president, walked past, stopping to tie his shoe. Corazon Aquino, President of the Philippines, sat toward the front, setting her purse on the seat beside her. (I wondered what a president needed a purse for.) Tariq Aziz, Deputy Prime Minister of Iraq, strolled by and smiled. Ted Turner came in with Jane Fonda and sat four rows further down. George H. W. Bush (the first George Bush, who was then the sitting American President) walked in and joined the American delegation. While ministers of 172 nation-states negotiated the text of Agenda 21, a blueprint for global environmental action, representatives of each country stated to the audience the challenges that sustainable development presented to their country: forest principles, financial resources, atmosphere, biodiversity and biotechnology, fresh water, technology transfer, desertification, population control, and all of the other challenges of ecology. The Marshal Islands' representative, for example, noted that his nation's seven-foot average elevation gave the country only a precarious grasp on life on an earth threatened with global warming.

After the first session, I asked Crystal, "What did you think?"

"I'm struck by the emergence I see of self-government."

"What?"

"Well, there are two conferences going on here—one made up of governments and one made up of people. I see the world ending up where each individual, guided by their Inner Voice, is self-governing."

"Wow! That's quite a visionary idea. But in a system where everyone's their own law, won't some people take advantage? What do you do about the bad guys?"

"There are two kinds of law, negative and positive. Governments are in business to enforce negative law: 'Thou shalt not.' They're doing the best they can, but governments are artificial entities, subject to the political influence of their millions of human constituents, each with a different, self-interested agenda. Individuals, who first and foremost have only themselves to answer to, are the creative, driving force behind all innovation, including environmental change. The individual creates the positive law in the world. I have always liked Margaret Mead's observation: 'Never doubt that a small group of thoughtful committed citizens can change the world;

indeed, it's the only thing that ever has.' Enriching the environment, instead of destroying it, is positive law."

"Where does positive law come from in each individual?"

"That's where the Inner Voice comes in. Government cannot legislate morality, as the saying goes—that must come from individuals. That's positive law."

"I'm not sure I get exactly what you mean."

"Think of the difference between Communism, with a central, controlled system, and capitalism, where the creativity of the individual is encouraged. All systems seem to benefit when individuals are self-governing. No government told Thomas Edison to invent the light bulb or Steve Jobs to assemble the Apple II, but it's those types of innovations that benefit all. Each individual's Inner Voice speaks to him about the important contribution each can make to benefit all. That's positive law. That's self-government. And I believe the world and each of its individuals will ultimately get there."

"Weren't Thomas Edison and Steve Jobs just trying to get rich?"

"Oh, I think there was more to it than that. Look at Gandhi (who started out as a litigator), Vincent Van Gogh, Boris Yeltsin, Nicola Tesla, the Dalai Lama, Mother Teresa, and all of the world's rich philanthropists who give their money away—they're all following their passion, not just grubbing for a little more money. If what they did made them money, fine. If it didn't, that was OK too so long as they had enough to get by and could express their vision. Following your passion, your inner fire, with or without money, is what brings happiness. How much governing do you think we'd need if everyone on earth was following his or her passion? Was happy?"

"Hmmm. Still, what do you do about the bad guys, the people intent on doing evil in the world?"

"Government performs critical functions at this point in our history, and maybe government will always be necessary or convenient. But I'm struck by the fact that individuals and their passion are the source of all sustainable development, not just ecology-wise. I'm reminded of our constitution which recites the functions of government—to establish justice, ensure domestic tranquility, provide for the common defense, etc.—but begins with the words, 'We, the People of the United States.' The Founding Fathers knew something about positive law."

"Aren't you mixing church and state?"

"Not at all; they're different worlds. 'Render unto Caesar the things which are Caesar's, and unto God the things that are God's.' We form governments to deal with common issues; but, historically, we've been most successful when we've kept government out of our personal relationship with the Universe. Government can't tell you how to be a good person...only how not to be a bad one. Wanting to be a good person and to make a positive contribution comes from within, from each person's unique connection to the Universe."

"Lots of political science at an ecology convention."

Crystal smiled. "Well, it's practical too. Think self-government. When you see something that needs doing, do it. When inspiration comes to take an action that benefits someone and harms no one, do it. Follow your own passion and everything will work out. That's how the Universe is hard-wired. That's positive law."

"I can just imagine the statute now: 'Thou shalt do whatever needs doing.'"

We both leaned back and laughed.

Later in the week, I met with my fellow ABA members attending the conference, all of whom seemed to be enjoying the back and forth negotiations by the various governments over the wording of Agenda 21, the blueprint for action to be adopted at the conference.

"We're making real progress on developing consensus for Agenda 21—more than we would if it were a treaty," Randall, one of the Chicago lawyers, said.

"What's the point of negotiating a consensus if it doesn't result in a treaty?" I asked.

"Well, first, Agenda 21 is 800 pages long and covers almost all of the issues relating to the world's environment. We would *never* get a treaty that broad ratified in more than a handful of countries. Second, the conference is looking to build on what happened after the 1972 Stockholm Convention—the consensus on an informal framework to deal with global environment issues developed at the Stockholm conference eventually solidified into international law. Treaties may be signed or not for political reasons, but international consensus on technology transfer, finance, and environmental dispute resolution has a way of developing into the way everyone does things and, ultimately, into international law."

"What happens with the governments that aren't participating in the consensus?"

"That's the incredible part about UNCED," Randall replied. "Everyone's here. For the first time in history, every important nation in the world was invited to a single meeting to solve a global problem, and every important nation came."

"Interesting point. So, how does this consensus get going?"

"The ministers of each country negotiate the terms of a conference statement of principles, like Agenda 21, during the main part of the conference. Then there is a final day or two of Plenary Sessions, where the leaders of the participating countries come to Rio and endorse the negotiated consensus in short speeches that are open to the public and news media."

"Other than government officials and the press, who actually gets to go to the Plenary Sessions?" I asked.

"Almost no one," was Randall's joking reply. "The speeches are all given in the main assembly hall and are attended by the countries' ministers and the press. Only 60 seats are reserved for the 2,400 appointed NGO representatives, and those are selected by the UN by geographic region. Of the 360 North American NGOs, only nine people get to go to the Plenary Sessions. The UN will *never* select the American Bar Association as one of the NGOs allowed to attend a Plenary Session; so you can be the one we choose to follow up on going to that!"

My fellow ABA representative was laughing and slapping me on the back as he mock-nominated me. As he did that, my thoughts raced back to the strong urge I had had to call the first ABA official to ask to be appointed as an ABA representative to UNCED; and then to the many serendipitous and magical things I had seen and done at the Earth Summit; and onward to the strong feeling I was *now* getting that I *would* be at the Plenary Session.

"Thank you," I said quietly to myself, knowing without the slightest factual foundation, or the slightest hesitation, that I would be there.

And so it was.

The next day the UN posted its list of authorized attendees, and my organization was on it. Upon seeing the list, I went immediately to the UN office to pick up the credential before anyone had a chance to change their mind.

When the time came for the event, I arrived early and wandered around in front of the main hall, where I came upon a large mural with foot-high script:

EARTH PLEDGE

Recognizing that people's actions toward nature and each other are the source of growing damage to the environmental resources needed to meet human needs and ensure survival and development,

I PLEDGE to act to the best of my ability to help make the Earth a secure and hospitable home for present and future generations.

The mural had thousands of signatures. As I got closer, I realized that one of the signatures on the mural was that of George H. W. Bush, the current American president I had seen earlier with the American delegation. *He didn't have to sign that*, I thought to myself. *I'm sure someone, somewhere, criticized him for signing the mural.*

But I knew that he had signed it as an air-breathing inhabitant of the planet, not as the head of the world's most powerful government. As I added my own signature to the mural, I thought of Marilyn's Earth Treaties, of Crystal's self-government, of positive law, of being inspired to make a contribution, or of simply following intuition and inspiration when it came along, like when it came for me in the urge to call that first ABA official.

The Plenary Session started and it was an incredible experience. In one day, in one meeting hall, the leaders of more than 50 percent of the world's population each personally delivered a similar message about a global problem—each as eloquently and succinctly put as it was that day by Fidel Castro, who declared we were in danger of losing an important species through loss of habitat: man.

The speakers in my session included Prime Minister Rao of India, Li Peng of China, Helmut Kohl of Germany, England's John Major, Brian Mulroney of Canada, Prince Rainier of Monaco, Fidel Castro, and the presidents of Portugal, Turkey, Argentina, Brazil, Morocco, and many other countries. George H. W. Bush spoke later in the day.

Looking back on it, I realize that I learned from the event that there was more to life than individual concerns about getting ahead; and that I wanted to be part of the solution and not part of the problem. This was the same decision that had been made by the many capable leaders I heard speak that day. Each of those global leaders, whether from Paraguay or Poland, was, in essence, just a regular person who was inspired to make a personal commitment to work with his neighbors, to live life as a "we," *we the people.*

CHAPTER TEN

POLONIA

"There is no love without forgiveness, and there is no forgiveness without love."—*Bryant H. McGill*

"Why don't you come along?" I heard my wife, Annie, say into the telephone.

Judging from the smile developing on Annie's face, I knew that my mother's immediate answer had been, "We'd love to!"

Annie and I were now middle-aged California lawyers, who for many years, had used our precious time off (and our frequent flier miles) from big-case law work to travel to many of the world's most interesting and beautiful places—so many countries that the pages of our passports barely had room for another stamp. This year, because Annie was full-blooded Lithuanian and because I was three-quarters Polish-German, and because we had been virtually everywhere else we wanted to go, we had decided to spend our vacation visiting our ancestral homelands in Central Europe.

Our itinerary had not yet been set when I called back home to wish my mother "Happy Mother's Day."

I spoke to her for a few minutes; then she passed the telephone with me on the line to my father; I passed him to Annie; and my father passed Annie back to my mother. Annie asked my mother what was happening in her life, and my mother asked Annie about the same. It was then that Annie talked to her about our planned trip to Central Europe. And, with the words "Why don't you come along?" our couple's vacation had suddenly turned into a four-person family excursion to Central Europe. Annie chatted some more, said goodbye to my mother, and hung up the telephone.

"Why did you invite my parents?" I asked.

"I'm sorry. It just popped out."

"Now we have to go. I can't tell them that you didn't ask me first. All of a sudden, it's a four-person family vacation with two people in their late 70s."

I loved my parents, but two weeks together, I thought, could be awkward, and anything but restful. Besides, Annie and I were not getting along all that well; and two weeks with just the two of us traveling together had, in the past, consistently brought us closer together. I figured we could use some intimate traveling time to smooth the bridge between us.

"Why not just enjoy it?" she said. "Or just cancel the whole thing, if that's the way you feel! If not, let's bring them along; it won't be any big deal."

When Annie's Lithuanian-born parents were alive, they had occasionally been included in various of our shorter trips, as had my parents on occasion. Her parents escaped from Lithuania during the First World War, settled in northern New Jersey, where her father operated a string of moderately successful small businesses, raised and educated three children—who became, respectively, a doctor, a computer network expert, and a lawyer—and lived a solid, thrifty, middle-class life. My father was the second of eight children, born of Polish émigrés to the United States in the early 1900s. Little was known of my father's parents' lives except for frightening stories about their having had to put my father and his older sister into orphanages while my grandmother battled pneumonia. Nonetheless, my grandmother ultimately raised eight children with my grandfather, who labored for a company building railroad cars. My mother was the second of four children, born to a second-generation German mother and a first generation Irish father, who (though color-blind) worked most of his life as a signal-electrician for the railroad. My parents had six children (one dying soon after birth), my father worked his entire career as a crane operator in the plant maintenance department of a Fortune 500 company, and my parents lived an upright, frugal life in Rochester, New York.

I did not answer Annie's comment about canceling the trip. Later, I meditated over what was happening here and formulated my questions: *Do I really want to spend this year's two vacation weeks traveling with my parents? Could I really cancel the trip entirely? Am I just resisting because Annie had made a unilateral offer that I couldn't, in good conscience, rescind? Why had Annie, on her own, turned a private time together into a close-quarters, four-person odyssey?*

The answer I got was to just go, that I would have a good time. Making the best of the situation, we made the arrangements and planned to meet my parents at JFK in New York and thereafter to fly to St. Petersburg,

Russia, Lithuania, and Poland before returning home. During the planning process, my father asked if the tour of Poland could include a trip to the general area of his father's birthplace, which he thought was near a place called Jaroslaw in southeastern Poland (my father didn't know where Grandmother was from in Poland). We passed the information along to a tour company in Warsaw that was arranging for a van and driver for us.

The month of May was very busy for me that year. I was lead counsel for European clients seeking to recover tens of millions of dollars in deposits and credits for equipment purchased from, but never delivered by, a large American manufacturer. The case was scheduled for trial in Los Angeles federal court, and opposing counsel were doing everything possible to derail our cause: selectively producing irrelevant documents and withholding critical ones; assigning 47 of their lawyers to generate daily objection paperwork requiring our response; scheduling work that had to be completed during Thanksgiving, Christmas, or other holidays; searching for reasons to contend that our side's European and American lawyers had violated court orders or Bar rules; seeking to disqualify our trial witnesses for conflicts of interest; and generally conducting the defense in the highest traditions of "trial by ordeal." I'll never know what dealings were done *behind* the scenes; but on June 3 of that year, I received a telephone call that the case had been settled. Suddenly, I had a lot of free time, which I was not eager to fill up with more work.

For the next week, I mostly slept, trying to rebuild what had been lost in month after month of 7-day weeks and 14-hour days. (By the end of May, I had already billed the firm's target hours for partners for the year!) For a few days after that, I pondered and meditated about whether I wanted to continue to expend the days of my life in the pressurized boredom of this grueling work. I decided to do nothing at all, until the day someone from the firm came by to ask me why I had stopped billing hours. In other words, I'd deal with it when that day came.

But the work pressure was now off; and the trip was planned, paid for, and would be awkward to cancel, particularly since I wasn't doing anything else. After very little deliberation, we decided to go forward with the trip. We met my parents at JFK in New York, flew to Russia, and on September 17, stepped off the plane together in St. Petersburg.

The intrigue and magic of international travel immediately began to unfold: customs officers in uniforms seem vaguely threatening because of associations drawn from long-forgotten Cold War movies; the appearance along the highway of all-black crows, like back home except for a strange shoulder shawl of furry white feathers; December-like cold and rain in September; temporarily being surrounded by the sounds of halting English (a language understandable even when spoken badly); our speaking a few words in Berlitz Russian, along with pantomime, to make ourselves understood; bland, heavy food in utilitarian hotels; the insane opulence of onion-domed Russian palaces from other eras; churches turned into government offices under the Communists, and thereby robbed of their sanctity; the wonder of The Hermitage museum with its astonishing collection of European modern art ("spoils of war," said the attendant, when Annie asked where the European art had come from); and the stalwart Russian people, dressed in coat and tie, high heels, and hats, as if to honor their beloved St. Petersburg with respectful, formal attire.

After three days, we were off to Lithuania, where Annie's parents had been born to shopkeepers in Vilnius, a beautiful old medieval city now surrounded by depressing Communist-era high-rise apartment buildings. However, in a petite blue, white, and yellow-decorated Old Town restaurant, which served excellent Parisian food accompanied by digital music from a white Yamaha Grand player piano, the enduring creativity of the people of this austere land peeked through the Communist-era clouds.

We looked through local telephone books for Annie's family name (shortened for use in America by her father and changed again to a common English-American name for use by one of her brothers). But Annie could not recognize the given names associated with her family's name; and, speaking no Lithuanian, we pursued the names and the "hunt for family" no further.

At the Vilnius airport, we prepared to board an AirPolonia Boeing 737 for the flight to Warsaw. We were flying business class, and AirPolonia loaded all of the other passengers before us. As our turn came, we were seated among the last eight rows of the aircraft. My mother turned to my father, and with a wink to us, said: "Only on Polish airlines do you have to pay extra to sit in the back."

We couldn't stop giggling about the absurdity of it during the short flight to Warsaw.

Once arriving in Warsaw, we find an old, recently rebuilt city now filled with entrepreneurs outlining deals on the backs of restaurant napkins. We visit the tourist stops and try some of the new restaurants that have emerged with the country's new commitment to private enterprise. But we sense that the soul of the country is in the countryside and the old capital, Krakow; so we eagerly look forward to the driving part of the Poland trip.

The tour company had organized a van and driver for us for the next four or five days, and we go to meet the driver, a solidly-built, mid-50s man wearing, always, a sport coat and dress pants. His wife is there too to see him off: same age, same heft, wearing a black dress that emphasizes her dyed-blonde hair. We motor away, and the driver soon establishes himself as an affable, sort-of-English-speaking, Polish everyman. As we drive south toward Krakow, he greets each of us, tells us that his name is Paul, that he is not a tour guide, because he only speaks a little English, but is happy to answer any questions that he can. He then drives along in easy silence.

My father engages Paul with his halting Polish, last spoken at home with his mother and father 70 years ago. Soon we are all asking the driver for the Polish words for "please," "thank you," "good day," and "How much does it cost?" My father starts to get into the game, speaking more and more Polish words dredged from long-unused parts of his memory. Paul chuckles and amiably supplies the proper Polish words for what my father's trying to say. They become a translation team—we ask my father a question; he repeats it to Paul using English and available Polish; Paul answers in the Polish and English available to him; and my father finishes the transition back into complete English. Somehow, it works! The mistakes are funny, and Paul becomes a member of the family, listening to our conversation in English and offering an occasional comment in English or Polish.

With hope in his voice, my father tells Paul the story of his father having come from southeastern Poland, perhaps from an area named Jaslo or Jaroslaw. Paul promises to drive through that area, after we've seen Krakow and Zakopane, a little resort town in the Carpathian Mountains near Poland's southern border.

We arrive in Krakow, Poland's old capital, the bishopric of Pope John Paul II and the home of the university where Copernicus invented modern astronomy. The tour operator has arranged for a guide who speaks excellent English to give us a tour of Krakow. We choose to call our guide "Rudy," since his Polish name is too difficult to pronounce easily. Rudy is an intelligent, energetic, early forties' man who is great fun ("My wife gets mad at how I introduce her: 'This is my first wife.'"). We walk the cobblestone streets where the Pope and Copernicus had walked, ending up in Market Square in the center of the old city, looking at the glorious, elegant architecture and the various stalls selling tourist trinkets. Rudy explains to us that "Polonia" (Poland) is a country of approximately 38 million people that, under the Communists, was semi-autonomous. During the Communist era, Russia had veto power over Polish policies but otherwise let Poland operate on its own. On the hour, we suddenly hear a trumpet playing from the tallest spire of a pink brick Gothic church in the square. We can see the live trumpeter playing the same thirty-second tune to each of the four directions; but each time, the tune abruptly ends on an eerie, broken note.

"Why?" I ask Rudy.

He explains. "The church was the Church of Our Lady, and, during the Middle Ages, a trumpeter played the 'Hejnal,' or 'Hymn to Our Lady,' from the same church tower on the hour to each of the four directions. One day, the trumpeter saw from his high-up stage an army of Russian Tartars on horseback galloping toward the city, apparently planning to sack it, as they had in the past. There was no time to get down off the church tower and try to warn the city of the imminent threat; so the trumpeter played the short hymn, not the usual four times, but very loudly and over and over and over again, until the people throughout the city realized that the urgent, repeated hymn was a warning and took action. The approaching Tartars also heard the repeated hymn; and when they got close enough, fired an arrow that struck the trumpeter's throat in mid-breath. To this day, the hymn is played and broken off at the same last note played by the trumpeter while saving his city."

It all seems so romantic and long ago, until I remember the empty Krakow Ghetto and the German concentration camps we saw on the way, which the Polish government preserves to silently dot the Polish countryside. (Auschwitz is just outside of Krakow.) What somber traditions this low-lying land has to remind its people of their ever-present, powerful neighbors! And thank you, America, for protecting us.

We turn from the church square to a restaurant in a little nearby hotel to have lunch with Paul and Rudy before seeing the rest of the city. After lunch, my father suddenly pulls an old envelope out of his trouser pocket and asks Rudy, "Can you read Polish?"

The envelope is yellowed with age and is one of those Old World weight-conserving kind that folds out, so the inside of the envelope becomes the blank page for writing. There are postmarks, stamps, addresses, and other indicators of place on the outside of the envelope, which was addressed to my grandmother, in her maiden name, at an address in Poland and had been forwarded to the United States.

"What's this?" Rudy asked.

"After my mother died, I found this letter when I was going through her things. From what little Polish I can read, it seems like it was written to her by a man who knew her in Poland. My mother's parents died from a plague when she was 12, and she was being raised by an uncle. When she was 16, there was no land or jobs in Poland to support them; so the uncle sent my mother and her brother Frank to Buffalo, New York, in 1907 to live in America."

"Well, let me see what I can do with it."

Scratching the side of his head, Rudy fixed his eyes intently upon the letter and began reading. "It's in old Polish," he quickly pointed out. "We don't use many of these words and spellings anymore."

Rudy continued to read the letter for maybe three minutes and then looked up. It was obvious he had started to become excited about this break from lecturing tourists about Krakow. Here was a 90-year-old letter written to a 16-year-old girl in Poland, kept among an old woman's things until the day she died at 88 in Rochester, New York, retrieved by her son and saved there in Rochester for another 17 years until it emerged from his pocket to be studied again by the old woman's descendants in a hotel in Krakow. Rudy knew, at that moment, that he was performing magic for us, that we treasured every word that he could eke out of the old letter.

"Let's move to the lobby where we can spread out and make some notes," he said. My mother, father, Annie, Paul, and I quickly moved to an open coffee table in the lobby and surrounded Rudy. As we sat down, my father pulled some more old documents from his pocket, including Grandmother's third grade report card, and set them on the low table. I lifted my camera to take a picture of this intent group; Rudy looked up again; and Paul began to study the old report card.

Returning his attention to the old letter, Rudy said, "Let's see—'Dear Mary'—'It's very cold this week'—"the letter is dated in February," he said. "'I've never

seen it this cold, and there's snow on the ground. I came by your uncle's house to see you, but no one was there.'"

"Is the letter signed by your father?" Rudy asked.

"No, no, my parents did not meet until they were both living in Buffalo, New York, and this is definitely not my father's name or signature. The letter looks like it was sent to my mother's old address in Poland and forwarded to her in Buffalo, New York. So, no, this letter looks like it was definitely written before my mother ever met my father."

"Was this a boyfriend?"

"I remember one of my nieces, Sherri, telling me that my mother had been very sympathetic toward her when Sherri had had her heart broken over a lost love when she was 16. Sherri said that grandma told her that the same thing had happened to her—so, yes, maybe this was a boyfriend."

Rudy continued to read and translate into English. "'I brought the gun to sell to your uncle, but no one was at the house. Did the family move? Did your uncle sell the farm? I came to see you about what we talked about. Please write to me as soon as you can to tell me where to reach you.'"

"The ending and signature are formal and correct," he added. "Let's look at the envelope." Studying the front of the envelope, Rudy called out the names of the places listed there: Grandmother's old address, the sender's address, and the location of the postage cancellation stamps.

"I can't tell exactly where these places are because the place names are small towns, and the names may have changed in the last ninety years."

My father tried to help by sharing something he remembered. "My mother always said that she grew up in Poland near the Ukraine border, about 60 miles from the Ukraine city of Lvov."

"That would put it in southeastern Poland. Where did you say your father was from?"

"It sounded like Jaslow, or Jaraslow, or something like that."

"Jaraslow is not far from the Ukraine border. Maybe the towns where your parents are from are near the Ukraine border, not that far apart. I'll give you the modern spellings of these place names so that you might recognize them if you drive through the area."

We thank Rudy profusely, and wonder at the appearance of this intelligent and capable man on our trip, right at this moment, to read us Grandmother's letter.

We continue on our way, visiting the ancient, and still then operating, salt mines at Wieliczka, a World Heritage site first mined in the 13th century. The rock salt from this place had been carved over the centuries into hundreds of underground frescoes, statues, sculptures, and even an underground cathedral. The ancient quarry is dark, warm, and filled with visions of industrious Middle Ages people laboring to create the civilization we now enjoy.

A few hours later, we arrive at Zakopane to find a pretty mountain resort town, reminding me a little of Ithaca, New York, with its steep streets, old houses, young people, and festive air. It starts to rain as we walk through the town to go to dinner. Suddenly, an open, horse-drawn carriage gallops up to where we're standing. The driver leaps off the carriage, says something in

Polish, thrusts the reins into my father's hands, and runs into the bar we're standing in front of. My father, a tall, spare man who spent his teens working on nearby farms, just laughs and holds the reins, comforting the panting horse. Within minutes, the wild-eyed driver bursts out of the bar, grabs the reins, says "thank you" in Polish, and gallops off, driving the horse way too fast, and weaving in and out among the cars on the rain-slick streets. My father laughs again and doesn't give it another thought.

But it causes me to think about my father. Seeing him on this trip, after years of working with expert witnesses in product liability cases, I realized that he had the mind of an engineer: logical, mechanically-oriented, inventive, solution-focused. He didn't waste time trying to change the system; he just dealt with what was there (making him an excellent card player). He had been a machinist's mate on submarines during the Second World War, tending to the diesel engines that powered the boat. I remember the family car repeatedly not starting for my mother once, years ago, and my father saying, "Oh, I'll just get some copper wire and rewire the generator to take care of that." It was years later before I knew how difficult it must have been to "just rewire the generator."

So, when a drunk gallops up and asks him to hold his horse while he gets another drink, "Sure, I see what your problem is; I can help with that," is what my father probably thinks. My mind works very differently, and unlike my father, I do fight to change the system, which caused endless misunderstanding between us.

My fighting the system included fighting the reign of my father as he raised his children, four of whom were boys. Raging against the system allowed me to become a lawyer instead of a supermarket clerk like many of the kids in my neighborhood. But it also did damage to the relationship between me and my father; perhaps necessarily so, given the differences in what we each expected out of life. When I got much older, I traveled to see my father in Rochester, New York, and asked for his forgiveness for that. He blinked, looked at me, and said, "Nothing to forgive." I only hope that, if my own son ever asks for forgiveness for the damage in our relationship, I have the wisdom and perspective to say, "Nothing to forgive."

Speaking of the terrible tradition of relationships between father and son in our family, it was clear to me during my childhood that my father did not like his father. My father worshipped his mother, always pointing out her many virtues, especially the unconditional love that even I remember pouring from her aging eyes. But my grandfather was apparently a different story. As a child, I heard wisps of tales about his being selfish, a womanizer, or being too busy to spend much time with each of his eight children. My father also occasionally complained that he didn't like the way my grandfather treated my grandmother. I do remember Grandfather calling Grandmother "woman;" but that seemed to be an acceptable way for husbands to address wives in the old country. When I was six or seven years old, my grandfather retired from the railroad and almost immediately had a stroke, which left him paralyzed on the left side and unable to speak clearly. This also left Grandmother with an invalid to wait on for many years, and I think my father resented that.

When we visited, conversations between my father and grandfather were short and strained: "Tommy, are you working?" "Is your car running?"

"Yes, Pa," my father would reply and turn to ask Grandmother if she needed help with anything. Grandfather would then look back toward the blaring television set, understanding that the conversation with his oldest son was over. Grandfather's Polish name was "Stanislas," Americanized to "Stanley." My father's given birth name was "Thomas Stanley;" but when I was growing up, he always signed his name "Thomas John."

Personally, I liked the old guy and he liked me, so much so that he gave me, of all of his grandchildren at that time, the watch that the railroad had given him when he retired. It was my first watch, and I wore it until it stopped working. I didn't like to look at the back of the watch case though. The railroad had engraved it but had spelled his last name wrong. It didn't seem to matter to him; but even then, I thought it symbolized the careless indifference with which these hard-working Polish people were dismissed at that time in America. I remember my father's brother telling me that Stanley had been the president of his local railroad workers' union; and I sometimes wondered whether I connected with my grandfather because, as a union leader, maybe like me and unlike my father, old Stanislas was a bit of a system-fighter too.

"Now, let's see about your father's place," Paul said to my father early the next morning, as he drove us out of Zakopane and toward Jaroslaw, the place name my father remembered as his father's old home in Poland.

As we motor along and play with the Polish words we're learning, I suddenly remember a word spoken as a curse by Polish relatives when I was young.

"What does 'hulera' mean?" I ask.

Instantly, my father responds: "Cholera." *Oh my*, I think, *what a serious curse, and what a comment on the dangers that beset this people.*

We drive along past rural houses with big, muscular women driving horse-drawn wagons that they're filling with beets and potatoes, which they're picking up in the fields.

My mother muses. "When I was little girl growing up outside of Rochester, New York, the girls were not expected to work in the fields." (That's news to me: Was I really *that* close to being sentenced to the life of a field hand?) The area we're driving through is near the Ukraine border and quite rural, but each house also has a satellite dish attached to one corner and, often, a small car in the driveway. I wonder to myself, *Is this really a late Middle Ages pastoral countryside or are these local people on the verge of an irreversible breakthrough to modernity?*

At about 9:00 in the morning, Paul announces that we're in Jaroslaw, a town of about 40,000 residents, although we certainly could not tell that by reading the signs, which are all in undecipherable Polish. Paul purposively drives to a government-looking building and starts to get out of the car.

"What is this?" I ask.

"Place of records," Paul replies.

We all pile into what looks like a county office, which apparently maintains records of the area's births and deaths. The government clerks smile when they see four Americans suddenly appear in their lives, and Paul begins speaking to them in Polish, pointing to my father and then to the rest of us, in order (wife, son, daughter-in-law). Paul asks my father a question in Polish, and my father answers, "1892 or 1893." Paul translates. The clerks smile again, and one scurries off, returning minutes later with a large, bound ledger. The clerk flips the pages and lands on "1892." There, the fifth entry down, May 3, 1892, is my grandfather's name.

My father asks Paul whether the clerks know where any relatives with my father's last name now live in the area. Paul speaks in Polish to the clerks. After some discussion among them, one of the clerks picks up the telephone, dials a number, speaks to someone on the other end of the line, and then tells Paul that people with that last name live a few kilometers away in a rural area called Zukow. Paul gets directions, we thank the clerks, and all of us exit the office building with a newfound ray of hope.

Once we're all back in the van, Paul drives toward Zukow, excitedly chattering with my father in Polish. We find a landmark mentioned in Paul's directions, an old, onion-domed church, where a country lane dead-ends into the road we're on. Turning into the country lane, Paul stops at the first house. He and my father jump out of the van and begin knocking on the house's front door. Their commotion attracts the attention of the occupants of the next house over, and two men in their forties stride to the connecting fence between the two houses and begin talking to Paul. We can piece together from the men's gestures that no one is home at the first house, that the fortyish men have the same surname as my grandfather, but that they are aware of no family connection to relatives in America. The men converse some more, then stop. Suddenly, one of the Polish men speaks excitedly. Paul and my father say "thank you" in Polish and hurry back to the van.

My father explains that the Polish man had said that he and my grandfather had the same last name but that the name was common in that area. However, that same man had suddenly remembered that he was distantly related to a farmer, Antonio, with the same family name, who lived seven or eight kilometers farther down the country lane. With huge grins on our faces, we dash off toward Antonio's farm!

Arriving at the right address for Antonio, we turn into a driveway with a small (1,000 square feet?), old, brick and stone house standing in front of an old stone barn. Paul and my father approach the front door and knock. The knock is answered by a young woman in her twenties, carrying what appears to be a two-year-old boy. Paul speaks to her in Polish. She then calls to a teenage boy, who listens intently to her and then runs off into the adjoining field. Shortly thereafter, the teenager returns with an early 80's man in hip boots, striding purposefully toward us.

My father shakes hands with the old man and starts to speak to him in Polish. Paul helps with the conversation, when necessary, and the dialogue continues. Suddenly, the old man says "Carl" and more words in Polish. My father repeats the name "Carl" and speaks more Polish to the old man. Then, they both stop speaking, and, still holding hands in the shaking position, look at each other for what seems a long time.

We later learned that the old man was Antonio, that his father (being the oldest son) had inherited the house and farm from his parents, that Antonio did indeed have aunts and uncles who had moved to America when Antonio's father inherited the farm in the early 1900s, that one such uncle had had a son, Carl, who had been killed in an industrial accident in Detroit in 1948. My father remembered that his father, Stanislas, had had a brother, Peter, who had a son, Carl, who had been killed in an industrial accident in Detroit in 1948. In an instant, these two old men suddenly realized that their fathers had been brothers, that Thomas' father, Stanislas, had thus been born in the very house we were standing next to, and that Antonio and Thomas were first cousins.

Antonio wastes no time in grasping the significance of the moment, as he immediately strides into the house and tells the young woman who had initially answered the door to make everyone breakfast, disregarding the apparent fact that we had all had breakfast hours earlier. Because of the personal nature of the situation, Paul demurs and politely offers to wait in the van, but Thomas and Antonio will have none of it—Paul is the clear communication link between the two cousins. Antonio introduces everyone: the young woman was his grandson's wife (his son had taken a factory job in the city instead of staying to work the family farm), and she had recently had their first great-grandchild. Antonio calls his babushka-bonneted wife, Aniela, from their quarters in the barn—the aging grandparents traditionally move into the barn to give the ancestral house to their children or grandchildren as they begin raising families; but the grandparents still own the land, and it seems, continue to rule the roost. (When Annie comments favorably on a string of wild mushrooms drying in the kitchen, Antonio picks them up and hands them to her to take back to Los Angeles.) The teenage boy is Antonio's grandson and, for agreeing to continue to work the family farm, has been, we are given to understand, designated to inherit it.

As the young woman begins to cook a breakfast of ham and eggs, my father suddenly says, "I want to pray," and begins saying grace. All of the people in the kitchen, Poles and Americans alike, know that my father's timing is a bit off but that he wants to somehow express his thanks to the universe for this wonderful, serendipitous meeting. Saying grace was the way he had found to express that thanks; so we all bow our heads too.

Antonio then goes out to change from his work clothes into his Sunday best. When he returns, he has a bottle of vodka in his hand and asks who wants to join him in a toast. Only my mother escapes the vodka toast—pointing out with a quick glance at her watch and polite refusal that it is 10:30 in the morning.

The talk continues during breakfast. My father asks, through Paul, if Antonio's family knows anything about my grandmother and where she was from. The Polish family shakes their heads, but Antonio suggests that he go back with us and raise that subject at the government office we had been at in Jaroslaw. Thinking this to be a splendid idea, we all pile back into the van and return to the Jaroslaw government office. When we get to Jaroslaw, my father, Paul, and I go into the office with Grandmother's old letter and Rudy's interpretation of the modern names of the places described on the envelope. The clerks recognize some of the names and direct us to the government records office in the next county over, about fifteen miles away, for directions to the exact places mentioned in the letter.

Antonio's farm was on the way, so Paul suggests that we drop Antonio off and continue. Antonio really wanted to participate in the next part of the adventure, but he understood that we had to move on (besides, Annie had refused his pantomime offer to go have a drink with him in a local bar while the rest of us were asking for directions in the government office). We drive back to his farm, and he tells us on the way that life had been better under the Communists. When I ask him, through Paul, to elaborate, he says it was because they took care of the farmers above all others, protecting them from the tyranny of market forces, such as those that had already driven his son to a factory job in the city. My father gives Antonio some folded bills, enough to thank him for receiving us graciously but not enough to be condescending.

As we were saying our last goodbyes at Antonio's

farm, the teenager drives up on a tractor. Antonio looks at him and says to my father in Polish: "Take him with you."

"To the next town?" my father asks.

"No, to America."

When the teenager realizes that Antonio is not joking, he scoffs loudly, no doubt mindful of his future inheritance of the farm. I wonder whether the boy had really thought about which was the bigger prize: inheriting this hardscrabble farm in Poland or not inheriting the farm and instead having to move to America, as my non-inheriting ancestors had done a century ago. The inheritor's descendants now eke out a living on the ancestral farm; the non-inheritors' descendants are lawyers. I know which life Antonio would choose now, if he had it to do over again. I feel empathy for the boy on the tractor, but I am also glad to get back into the van.

On the drive to the next government office, we jabber away, buoyed by anticipation about this experience of connecting with a first cousin of my father. I wonder, *Can we also find something out about Grandmother's family?*

The clerks we meet when we arrive at the county government office, in a town somewhat bigger than Jaroslaw, are more reserved; but they also quickly produce the ledger for my grandmother's birth year, 1891. And there, next to November 3, is my grandmother's name, along with the names of her parents! This sparks a memory of the names from my father when he read his maternal grandparents' names in the ledger. He asks, with Paul's help, "Do you know where descendants of that family live today?"

Unfortunately, their answer is, "No." Grandmother's family name was common here and across the nearby Ukrainian border. If the farm was sold a century ago, it would be impossible to know which people with Grandmother's family name were closely related to her.

A few minutes after we drive away from the government building through the town, Annie suddenly says, "Turn here."

We all look at her quizzically, but Paul quickly makes the turn. As we drive along the new street, I suddenly spot Grandmother's family name above the postal slot on one of the houses.

"There's her name," I exclaim, "Right at this driveway!"

Paul pulls into the driveway, stops behind an old Fiat, and gets out with my father to knock on the door. The knock is answered by a woman in her early thirties, to whom Paul and my father explain the reason for our visit. She invites us in and calls into another room for her father-in-law, a man in his mid seventies, who quickly joined the conversation. The old man does not recognize Grandmother's first and middle names; but he asks the young woman to bring the family photo album. He opens the album to the oldest pictures—formal shots taken out-of-doors, with the men in turn-of-the-century suits and ties and the women and children in Sunday wear.

Suddenly, my father exclaims, "Cha Cha Lavinia!" He had noticed in one of the old pictures an aunt ("Cha Cha" means "auntie" in Polish) he recognized from his childhood in Buffalo, New York. The woman identified in the old picture was a large woman in her late twenties, with a mischievous smile on her face. My father and the old man excitedly confirm that this was the same loud jokester with a big heart who they both had known—the old man while in Poland and my father while in New York—after she had emigrated to the United States. My father said that Cha Cha Lavinia (I remembered relatives talking about her when I was a child) was his mother's sister, and the old man said that she was his father's cousin; and so the exact family relationship was established!

The front door to the house then opens, as if choreographed, and the old man's son, the young woman's husband, walks in for his daily lunch break from his factory job. His wife quickly explains what was happening, and he suggests that we all drive to the cemetery to visit the graves of my grandmother's relatives, which he could readily identify through the common links with Cha Cha Lavinia and the other people in the old picture. We walk to the vehicles ("Let's take the van," the son says. "The Fiat has a flat."). When we get to the cemetery, the son takes us to the relevant sites, a peoples' genealogy expressed in headstones and remembered funerals. My father stands over and ponders each site.

We thank our gracious hosts and drive on, marveling at how we would *never* have found this place unless my father had brought Grandmother's old letter to Krakow, Paul had gotten us to Narol, Annie had gotten the intuition to turn down a street in an unfamiliar town in rural Poland, I had spotted a familiar nameplate, *and* Cha Cha Lavinia had made such a strong impression on all touched by her boisterous humor nearly a century ago!

We ended up a few days later back in Warsaw. Paul went home but returned the next day with gifts to see us off on our flights back to the United States. And yes, when we got back to Los Angeles, we did cook and eat the mushrooms Antonio gave Annie, with no ill effects.

Things happened quickly after we returned: I left my law work to become a writer; Annie and I separated within six months of the trip; my mother died within a year; and my heartbroken father died a few years after that. We all talked often of the trip because it seemed like it had been arranged by the universe for each of us to say goodbye to those people with whom our work together on this earth was coming to an end. We each contributed our designated part to the success of the adventure, and we each understood the others a little better because of the trip.

I remember that in the months that followed the trip, my father sent thank you notes to us and letters to the English-speaking descendants of Antonio in Poland, to whom he wrote: "I would like to tell you that going to the place of my father's birth and meeting my relatives was one of the great experiences of my life."

And those letters, like all of my father's documents from then on, until the day he died, were all signed "Thomas Stanley," not "Thomas John."

A healing, on many levels, had taken place in Polonia.

CHAPTER ELEVEN

HEALING

> "The greatest healing therapy is friendship and love."—Hubert H. Humphrey

"Jay's in the hospital," Tom said. "They think he might have appendicitis."

It was a typical, busy Monday morning at my Los Angeles law office. Tom, my son's college roommate, was calling from Tucson.

"What happened?" I asked, feeling the slow dread that comes to any parent with a hospitalized child.

"Jay had a stomach ache on Sunday night; and when we got up this morning, it just got worse and worse. So I finally took him to the emergency room. The doctors did some tests and found out that his white blood cell count was elevated. They admitted him to the hospital, and a gastroenterologist is on the way over to look at him now. But he seems pretty sick."

"Thanks for taking Jay to the hospital, Tom. Tell him I'll be there today, as soon as I can, and I'll call you, Tom, when I have some flight information."

"No problem."

I got off the line with Tom and dialed my wife. "Hi, Annie. How would you like to have lunch in Tucson today? Tom just called and said that Jay's in the hospital with a stomach problem that might be appendicitis."

"Oh, no," Annie said. "Sure, when can we get there?"

"I'll ask my secretary to book a flight to Tucson while we're driving to the airport. I'll be over in front of your office in about ten minutes."

There were frequent flights between Los Angeles and Phoenix, and we were able to leave as soon as we got to the airport. Since it was August, it was over 110 degrees Fahrenheit when we rented a car in Phoenix and began the 100-mile drive to Tucson. Halfway to Tucson, one of Arizona's famous "monsoon" storms drifted into our path and pelted us with rain for a few miles. Even more impressive than the rain was the sudden, twenty-degree drop in temperature caused by the monsoon.

"Can you imagine the energy it takes to cool a thousand square miles of air down by twenty degrees in a few minutes?" I remarked to Annie.

"Yes, that's incredible! And the energy it takes to heat it right back up again when the sun comes out."

And that's what had happened by the time we got to Tucson.

When we arrived at the hospital, the nurse on duty told us that the gastroenterologist had already seen Jay and had tentatively concluded that Jay probably had appendicitis. He was in great pain, and the doctor had put him on morphine. We went in to see Jay.

"How are you feeling?"

"It hurts *so bad*," he said in a way that I knew from

raising him for the past 23 years meant that he was *not* acting.

"What did the doctor say?"

"He said that they'll take some more tests later today, but that they'll probably have to operate on me tomorrow morning."

"My poor baby," I said, only half-joking. Jay didn't even smile.

"Please make it better," he said. "It hurts *real* bad." I looked at Annie. We had been studying with Crystal, who had helped us recognize that love is divine energy and that sending love to a person could assist in their healing. We were standing in a hospital room in Tucson with a sick person we loved, and there was nothing else we could do for him. *Why not try a healing?* I thought.

"Jay, what if we tried to make it better by asking for healing?"

"*Anything* to make it better."

Now, a lot of Crystal's teaching was practical advice about handling life's day-to-day issues in a positive, instead of a destructive, manner. Much of her teaching, however, was about each individual's relationship with the universe, including the possibility of accessing healing energies. Could such energies be as real as the energy of the rainstorm we had just driven through? I really don't know how much of the teachings Annie and I wholeheartedly believed and how much we were just observing without commitment. I *do* know that the teachings helped us become better people, more tolerant of others, more compassionate, and less prone to anger. Jay had seen us become calmer about life after studying with Crystal; and even if he didn't subscribe to the course we were taking, he had kept an open mind. He was in obvious pain and at this point was not ruling out anything that would help.

"Let's try it, then," I said. Annie nodded in agreement.

Making it up as we went along, I held my hands a few inches above Jay's abdomen, closed my eyes, and sent love from my heart into Jay's abdomen. I held in my mind the thought, "I AM healed." Annie "held the Light" for Jay (meaning, she mentally surrounded him with a loving white light). This "process" only lasted a few moments, and during it, nothing was said out loud. But the entire room seemed enlivened and full of love, hope, and optimism for Jay. Annie and I opened our eyes and laughed a nervous laugh.

"We didn't get the address information for the gastroenterologist," I said. "The nurse outside probably has it. Let's check with her and see." Annie and I went out to talk to the nurse.

When we walked back into the room, Jay was sitting up, watching television, and eating from a bowl of ice cream that had been left over from his previously untouched lunch. He smiled when we walked in.

"I feel a lot better!" he said. Jay slept soundly that afternoon and evening and seemed completely better the next morning.

We met with the gastroenterologist in the morning, who said, "Jay's white blood cell count is now well within the normal range, he's pain free, and he has no other symptoms of appendicitis. My instinct is to not operate and see if Jay's infection just resolves on its own. There's always some risk with surgery; and if it can be avoided, all the better."

The final decision—which took into account the opinion of the gastroenterologist—was to avoid surgery. Within a few hours' time, Jay went back to life as a college student, and we were all left wondering what had happened in that hospital room in Tucson. Later, when Annie and I discussed this "event" with Crystal, she said that we "were very much a part of the healing" of Jay. Our doubts persisted, however. Were we supposed to believe that two lawyers had anything to do with healing appendicitis in a college student who was lying in a hospital, attended to by highly trained medical specialists? Annie and I were puzzled.

A seemingly odd confirmation of what had happened in Tucson occurred a few days later. We often went out to dinner in Santa Monica and would, like most people, ask for take-out boxes for the portions of the meals we couldn't finish. As we'd walk from the various restaurants toward wherever our car was parked, we would often pass by homeless persons on the street. Typically, we'd offer them the food, which they invariably took. During the past year, we had run into an unusual old homeless woman, whom we had spoken to on occasion. The woman would approach people on the street and offer to sell them a bouquet of flowers that she had just salvaged from wherever they had been discarded. The flowers were always wilted and looked like they had come from the trash, which, of course, they had. It was an obviously absurd sales proposition, but the woman kept at it quite good-naturedly; as if someone would actually *want* to buy her faded bouquets. Once, the old woman approached Annie and offered to sell her a bouquet.

Annie said, "I don't want any flowers right now; but would you like to have some food?" handing our take-out box toward the old woman.

The woman smiled and said, "What is it?"

"Carnitas," Annie replied.

"Oh, I don't eat meat. But I have a friend who does, and I'll take the food."

"Why don't you eat meat?" Annie, herself a vegetarian, asked.

"It's not good for you, and it involves killing animals," the old woman said, smiling.

We talked with her a little and found her to be a delightful old woman, obviously intelligent, and completely untroubled by the inconsistency of a homeless person being fussy about her health. Every time we saw her after that, we would offer her our leftovers, which she always accepted, shifting the decrepit bouquets she often carried to the other hand, in order to take the boxes.

We hadn't seen the old woman for several months before our sudden Monday trip to visit Jay in the hospital in Tucson; but when we finished dinner on the Saturday following that trip, she suddenly appeared, carrying her usual bouquet. Annie went up to her and gave her the food.

"Would you like to buy some flowers?"

Annie said she didn't want any flowers tonight but gave the old woman $5.

"Thank you. It was very hot in Tucson this week, wasn't it?"

"How did you know I was in Tucson this week?" Annie asked, startled.

The old woman just smiled and said, "Oh, I know things."

We never saw the old woman again, but I often wondered if the universe had given us some sign to pay attention to about the healing in Tucson through the old woman in Santa Monica. In giving food to the old woman, had we "thereby entertained an angel unawares"?

We had another opportunity to try healing within a few days of the trip to Tucson. One of our friends was a Native American songwriter who was staying with us for a few days. His girlfriend had come over to visit, and they had gotten into some argument. She started to leave and got into her little sports car, with him leaning on her door, asking her to stay. They had some more words; suddenly she started the car and drove off—right over his foot! He only had moccasins on, and the foot began to become black and blue and immediately swollen. Being a spiritual person, he promptly asked us for healing. After Annie put ice on his foot, we performed the same type of healing ceremony that we had done a few days earlier in Tucson. To everyone's surprise, the swelling stopped, the pain went away, and our friend began walking normally on the injured foot, right away!

In the coming months, I tried healing on myself several times. One cold lasted thirty-six hours, instead of a week as it usually did. Cramps caused by an intestinal virus in Mexico City cleared up overnight. Another cold resolved in a few hours, leaving me feeling fine except for the leaden effect of the cold remedies I had taken to alleviate the symptoms.

At other times, however, I seemed to have no access at *all* to healing energies: colds raged on unabated; the flu ran its course without interruption. Jay eventually *did* have his appendix out, two years after the event in Tucson; and I stopped thinking about healing, even though our spiritual teacher kept saying that I could be a conduit for healing if I wanted to be.

Several years later, everything in my life had changed, and I had moved to California's central coast with Lauren. I also had completely forgotten about healing. Then, one day in 2001, Lauren and I stopped by the house of an interior designer we were working with to drop something off. As Lauren turned away from the front door to leave, her foot missed the step, and she fell heavily, obviously injuring her right foot. It began swelling immediately, and she winced with pain. The local emergency room was only a few minutes away, but I got the strong feeling that we should try to heal her foot before driving there and before we knew what any X-rays would show. I asked Lauren if she wanted to try the healing or go immediately to the emergency room, without pausing.

"No, let's do the healing first," Lauren said. "Let's ask that it only be muscles that are damaged, but no broken bones."

We did the healing ceremony quickly. Lauren closed her eyes and mentally asked her angels for healing. At the same time, I held my hands just above the swelling, closed my eyes, and mentally sent love from my heart through my hands into Lauren's injury, while holding the thought, "I AM healed."

Once we were "done," I helped Lauren into the car, and we drove over to the hospital. The X-rays came back negative; Lauren was fitted with a boot cast, and the muscles eventually all healed. But I always wondered whether, if we had not done the healing ceremony before we knew what the X-rays showed, we would not have believed that broken bones could be repaired in a healing ceremony, and Lauren would have ended up with broken bones and not just the lesser muscle damage that we had "asked for." Regardless, after that incident, I found my interest in healing returning.

Around that time, my father had developed a medical condition that steadily worsened, until he had become confined to bed. My father had had a long, successful marriage with my mother, and when she died, he seemed to lose the will to live. I remember asking him once, during a telephone call, what he was doing for the rest of the day.

"I thought I would go play cards with George in the morning, get some groceries," he said, "then go back to the house and sit."

Although he had been physically healthy through most of his life, he had recently developed asbestosis from smoking cigarettes and working around industrial construction sites for many years. When he learned that he had the disease, he asked me to arrange to have a will written, which I did, leaving what little property he had equally to his five children. He was being cared for magnificently by my youngest brother, but it was clear that the end was in sight. I traveled with another of my brothers from Los Angeles to Rochester, where my father lived, to visit one last time. When we arrived at the house, my youngest brother told us, before we saw our father, that he was on morphine for the pain but was otherwise quite lucid. My father asked for a few moments to get situated, and we went in to see him when he was ready. It was a shock—a man I remember as being able to consistently ring the bell with a sledge hammer at the local county fair contests now was lying in bed with atrophying muscles in his once-powerful arms.

"Hi, Dad, I'm glad to be here," I said. "Is there anything I can do for you?"

He looked at me, laughed a little, and said, "You could heal me."

Bam! Right there, the universe put the proposition to me: *Are you a healer or aren't you?* I wondered to myself, *What if I do a healing ceremony, and I can't heal my father? And what if I can?* I knew that my father missed my mother terribly, that he was at about the age when his own parents had died, and that he probably did not want to live. *What should I do with my father's piercing comment?* I'm sure he meant it as a wry little joke to comfort me, but how far should I push my growing feeling that I *could* be a conduit for healing energy?

I elected to do nothing and just said, "Oh, how are you feeling right now?" My father responded, and we went on to have our last visit together. He died within a few months. In discussing it later, a spiritual teacher suggested that I might have answered my father's question with one of my own, "Do you want to be healed?" I wish I had—I'm sure his answer would have been, "Not really." He was honest enough of a man to say just that, and the decision of whether to push it any further would have been made for me. But I often later wondered: *Why did he make that comment? Should I ask someone what they really want before ever trying to access healing energy? What does "the patient" believe about healing? What do I believe about healing?*

I knew from the sporadic healings I had witnessed that it was useless to predict healing or to understand which supplications resulted in healing and which were met with no apparent result. What seemed to work best was to listen, without judgment, to the essence of the request, to ask for the healing, and to move on regardless of the result, remembering at all times that I was not doing the healing, just the asking.

During the following year, I had an occasion to call the office of the interior designer on whose step Lauren had the previous incident. The office personnel related that Michael, the interior designer, was sick and would be recuperating at home for the next few days. We knew from past experience that Michael was prone to sickness, especially when he needed time off that he couldn't justify to himself taking in any other way. We also knew that he lived alone and could spiral down into a dark mood that was hard for him to shake off when he got sick. After lunch that day, it suddenly occurred to me to buy some "Get Well" balloons, bring them over to his house, and try to cheer him up a little. Lauren immediately got into the fun of it and suggested a place where we could get the balloons, which we did on the way over to his house.

When we arrived with the balloons, Michael was delighted and shocked that we had taken the trouble to come by. He invited us to come out and sit in his backyard, which he had beautifully landscaped into a quiet retreat with a gurgling water fountain. We gave him the many colored balloons, which he held onto tightly. We talked about his illness, and he said that he felt a little better already.

Lauren got the idea to ask, "Would you like us to do a healing?"

"Sure, I'd love it," he replied. Michael's parents had two daughters, and eleven years later, had him. Michael's father had died when he was young, and being effectively an only child at that point, the boy spent a lot of time alone. He developed a method of coping with the world completely through feelings, rather than through the intellect, which made him a great designer. It also, however, made him vulnerable to any negative, or positive, feelings that came his way.

Making it up as we went along, we asked that Michael be healed and sent him love from our hearts. Suddenly, we all began to feel what I can only describe as a swirl of energy, as if time had stopped, and the only universe in existence was the backyard where the three of us were asking for healing for Michael. It was a powerful moment—the three of us suspended together in some bubble of healing energy, as if we had temporarily ascended into a loving eternity, where all outcomes were possible.

It was one of only a few times in my life when I felt that sort of swirling energy, or "buzzing," as if I was energetically connected with the power of the universe: once before with Lauren, as we were saying a reluctant goodbye at an airport; once during my law career, when I realized, as it was happening, that I was being presented with the opportunity of a lifetime and that I knew exactly what to do with it; and this time with Michael. As we were getting up to leave, a neighbor of Michael's called over to him, as she was leaving her house, to ask how he was feeling. He bounded up and practically sprinted over to greet her, still clutching the "Get Well" balloons in his left hand.

From time to time after that, whenever the occasion arose, Lauren and I would ask for a healing. Sometimes it worked. Oftentimes, it apparently didn't. We continued to go to doctors, with their magnificent diagnostic tools; but although we listened to what the doctors had to say, we only followed their advice when it resonated with what we were feeling was right. And this "practice" seemed to work: we were rarely sick, and following our intuition about the doctors' advice had yet to prove to be a mistake.

Being novices, we decided to research a little about what the world thought about healing through intention. We quickly found records of thousands of years of history on the subject, and this insightful defense of the concept written by the noted Harvard psychologist, William James, over 100 years ago:

> ...[quoting a contemporary psychologist] 'In spite of the severe criticism we have made of reports of cure, there still remains a vast amount of material, showing a powerful influence of the mind in disease. Many cases are of diseases that have been diagnosed and treated by the best physicians of the country or which prominent hospitals have tried their hand at curing, but without success. People of culture and education have been treated by this method with satisfactory results. Diseases of long standing have been ameliorated, and even cured...

We have traced the mental element through primitive medicine and folk-medicine of today, patent medicine, and witchcraft. We are convinced that it is impossible to account for the existence of these practices, if they did not cure disease, and that if they cured disease, it must have been the mental element that was effective... It is true that many failures are recorded, but that only adds to the argument. There must be many and striking successes to counterbalance the failures, otherwise the failures would have ended the delusion.'

William James, *The Varieties of Religious Experience*, (New York: The Modern Library, 1902), 95, quoting H.H. Goddard, "the Effects of Mind on Body as Evidenced by Faith Cures," *American Journal of Psychology* (1899), (vol. x).

In short, if healing through intention did not work, it could not have survived in the world as long as it has.

Professor James went on to compare scientific healing and healing through intention:

> Science gives to all of us telegraphy, electric lighting, and diagnosis, and succeeds in preventing and curing a certain amount of disease. Religion in the shape of mind-cure gives to some of us serenity, moral poise, and happiness, and prevents certain forms of disease as well as science does or even better in a certain class of persons. Evidently, then, the science and the religion are both of them genuine keys for unlocking the world's treasure-house to him who can use either of them practically. Just

as evidently neither is exhaustive or exclusive of the other's simultaneous use. And why, after all, may not the world be so complex as to consist of many interpenetrating spheres of reality, which we can thus approach in alternation by using different conceptions and assuming different attitudes, just as mathematicians handle the same numerical and spatial facts by geometry, by analytical geometry, by algebra, by the calculus, or by quaternions, and each time come out right? On this view religion and science, each verified in its own way from hour to hour and from life to life, would be co-eternal. Primitive thought, with its belief in individualized personal forces, seems at any rate as far as ever from being driven by science from the field today. Numbers of educated people still find it the directest experimental channel by which to carry on their intercourse with reality.

Ibid., pp.120-1.

Our further research into where medicine stood these days revealed that the contemporary medical establishment was itself beginning to accept the non-physical side of healing described by William James a century ago. Traditional medicine involved diagnosing, treating, or preventing damage to the body or mind, as if the body were a machine, like a watch that needed repair. Doctors did things "to" the body. But times were changing. The well-documented "placebo effect" suggested that humans have a strong "mind-body" connection and that one can heal one's own body through desire, expectancy, and belief in healing. More recently, medicine had begun to consider the possibility that one person could heal others' bodies through the power of focused intention—healing. Studies in quantum physics suggested that all reality is comprised merely of energy and information, that the energy is all connected, that reality can be changed by subtle alterations in energy, and that human focus can interact with the quantum field. *Why not healing through intention?*

Did I really believe it? I wasn't really sure, until quite recently. I had come to know a "life coach," Hope, a spunky little woman who regularly held classes in different parts of the country for people who wanted her help with doing things a little better in their already-successful lives—like communicating better, making choices more consciously, living more authentically, and taking other practical steps for a happier life. Hope believed that our bodies are delicate instruments that create feelings and symptoms of illness to tell us to change things in our lives that had gotten out of balance. Part of her coaching was to make the first response to any symptom an "inquiry" into what the patient could change in their life to eliminate the cause of the symptom. Then, she would ask for healing for the patient. She was far and away the healthiest eighty-year-old I had ever met.

One day a few years ago, Hope telephoned me and asked for healing for a cold she felt coming on. I promptly did a healing ceremony, and she called back to say that her cold was gone. After that, she would call whenever she or one of her many students was in discomfort. On many occasions, she would call back to say "thank you" on behalf of the now-comfortable person.

A few months ago I contracted an intestinal virus that started as a backache and then turned into a stomach ache *so* painful that I could not eat. I tried a healing on myself, but nothing happened, and the pain got worse. Between the backache and the stomach ache, there was soon no position that was comfortable. Sitting at the kitchen table, trying to read the newspaper in agony, the thought occurred to me to call Hope and ask for a healing for me. I made the call, and she agreed to do it. Hanging up the telephone, I continued to turn the pages of the newspaper until I came upon an interesting article, which I started reading. Ten minutes into the article, I suddenly realized that my pain, although not completely gone, was greatly diminished, *and* that I was actually comfortable in my seated position! That moment marked the turning point for the virus, and in a day or two, it was completely gone. I called Hope as soon as I realized that something had happened immediately after I had asked for her healing help.

"Thanks very much," I said. "I wonder why the relief happened so quickly."

"Maybe it was time for you to experience being on the receiving end," she replied.

I became a better "believer" after that experience. Now, I explore in earnest this magic "worm hole" in the energy universe that sometimes—inexplicably, miraculously, thankfully—results in healing.

CHAPTER TWELVE

THANKSGIVING IN SAN FRANCISCO

"Whatever we think about and thank about
we bring about."—*John F. DeMartini*

"Did you say go to San Francisco for Thanksgiving?" Lauren asked.

"Sure," I said, "Why don't we make something exciting happen with Thanksgiving for once? Besides, being out of town would avoid all of the questions about whether we're going to spend Thanksgiving with relatives, eating a big meal, and watching football games."

"Will anything be open? Will there be anything to do there? I like football games."

"We'll find something to do. It'll be fun to just go and see what we can make happen."

"Well, I'm willing to try it. Can we get hotel reservations?"

"On Thanksgiving and the day before, no one is going to be staying overnight in San Francisco. So, yes, I think we can make that happen."

We lived in Hearst Castle country, halfway between Los Angeles and San Francisco. It was an easy 235-mile,

3-½-hour drive to San Francisco from our house overlooking Edna Valley in San Luis Obispo.

We made the drive many times a year to balance the semi-rural life that we loved with the cultural, culinary, and civilized delights only a major city can provide. So we knew the ebb and flow of hotel availability and rates in San Francisco and were able to make the arrangements happen quickly.

We got up early the Wednesday morning before Thanksgiving and began the drive to San Francisco through one of the most historic, yet least known, parts of California. I like this drive for its beauty *and* for the romance of its colorful history, which continues to unfold right down to this very day.

In 1775, Juan Bautista de Anza led a colonizing expedition of thirty families of married soldiers, from what is now Tubac in Southern Arizona to found a presidio (or military fortress) and mission near the San Francisco

Bay. The path they, and many others later, took through coastal California became known as "El Camino Real" (Spanish for "The King's Highway"), and it is today known as US 101, the freeway we take to travel to San Francisco. The 125-mile stretch of US 101 we drive on from San Luis Obispo to Salinas was built 50 years ago by Alex Madonna, a San Luis Obispo native of Italian-Swiss descent, who became a wealthy local celebrity with Hollywood connections. He also built the Madonna Inn, a large, kitschy, Swiss-Alp themed, pink inn decorated with all of the fussy, yet precise, touches with which the Swiss festoon their creations. The Madonna Inn is built right off of a US 101 exit and is a mandatory restaurant stop for the many tour buses that drive that freeway. It is also a local landmark and considered "the proper place" for any local family function. At any birthday celebration for Sumuko, Lauren's mother, Alex, who had gone to high school with one of Sumuko's many sisters and knew her extended family, would stop by the table, have his picture taken with the celebrating family, and send over one of the Inn's colossal and famously delicious cakes for dessert.

San Luis Obispo itself has a long history, growing from its start in 1772 as the third of the 21 California missions (linked by El Camino Real) founded by Father Junipero Serra. In addition to the early Spanish settlers, Chinese laborers were brought in to build the railroads, Portuguese sailors fished the local waters, and Japanese railroad laborers stayed to become successful area farmers. In fact, Lauren's grandfather, to whom a San Luis Obispo city park was recently dedicated, came to America when his older brother inherited the family farm in Japan, worked for the railroad to develop some capital, bought and cleared some land for a farm near the ocean, and in 1918 started only the third family to live in a nearby coastal town that today has 14,000 residents.

It's notable that this long line of immigrating people has, apparently, so seamlessly blended into the local American melting pot: at the annual Paso Robles Mid-State Fair, local Anglo cowboys can be seen chatting amiably with their Asian high school classmates, both eating Portuguese linguica sausage cooked by a chef whose last name is Torres. When Lauren's entire family was interned during World War II for being Japanese and living too close to the open ocean, her grandfather's Anglo neighbors watched over his farm to make sure that it would still be his when he got out of the prison in New Mexico, to which he had been sent by the federal government.

So, when second generation Swiss Alex sends a "thanks for your business" dessert cake over to the table of second generation Sumuko, her third generation Japanese-American children and their spouses (including a dash of third generation Polish-American), an American Thanksgiving is renewed against the backdrop of hundreds of years of living history.

Our drive up to San Francisco parallels the San Andreas Fault, as it divides the coastal portion of California that rests on the Pacific Plate from the rest of the United States. En route to our destination, we continue to follow the Fault right past the old Spanish missions at Carmel (where Padre Serra is buried) and San Juan Bautista, and then through Silicon Valley, where we switch from US 101 to Interstate 280. By changing highways, we take advantage of the magnificent redwood forest scenery, the view of San Andreas Lake in the San Andreas Rift Valley, and the southern entry into San Francisco.

Lauren and I discuss that San Francisco has been blessed and cursed by the San Andreas Fault: "blessed" when it created San Francisco Bay and its dramatic physical setting, by pushing the coast down and letting the Pacific Ocean flood a series of inland tectonic valleys; and "cursed" by the fault when it destroyed San Francisco in 1906 (as it will likely again some day do).

We also talk about the enduring magnetic pull this area has had on the citizens of the world: first through the gold rush of 1849; then, through the commerce generated by one of the world's greatest natural ports; now, through the technological revolution pulsating in Silicon Valley; and always, through the everlasting beauty of the area. San Francisco has attracted people from every country on earth: 30% of the city's population is Asian; its Chinatown is the largest outside of Asia; and 15 million people visit San Francisco every year. A cab ride in the city is often an ethnic adventure, with drivers' radios playing music from a wide variety of "homelands"—in one series of cab rides, in one day, we heard music from Russia, Syria, Romania, Jamaica, China, and Iran!

One result of the city's immigrant diversity and energy is a passionate competition in its thriving restaurant industry. Not only are there restaurants from every conceivable ethnic tradition, but there is also, among those restaurants, a high level of creativity and commitment to culinary excellence. One of the best, a dim sum "parlor" (as they are affectionately known), is our first stop in San Francisco.

Dim sum is a Canton Chinese expression variously translated to mean "order to one's heart's content," "touch the heart," or simply "snack." What it refers to (as many have discovered to their delight) is a variety of small, hot dishes, eaten while drinking tea in the late morning or early afternoon. The dishes, each comprised of three or more individual pieces on a small plate, brought continuously from the kitchen through the restaurant on rolling carts, are small rice or wheat flour dumplings, filled with the primary ingredients for that dish: barbeque pork, shrimp, chive, egg custard, or any of dozens of other ingredients. Dim sum left the relatively bland confines of Cantonese cuisine when it arrived in Hong Kong—another city by a bay with a commitment to culinary excellence—to be reinterpreted by the many chefs from all over China who gravitated to that international city in the South China Sea. Hong Kong added spice, fire, and creativity to dim sum, turning it into a dish best made fresh, served steaming hot, and powerfully, yet delicately, seasoned. Assembling the fresh primary ingredients, inserting the ingredients into a delicate rice flour skin, seasoning the dumplings perfectly, steaming them the optimum amount of time, and continuously serving the dishes hot is quite a difficult feat, and few restaurants anywhere in the world excel at it. The owner of our favorite dim sum parlor once told us that he had nine chefs on staff to keep the endless stream of perfectly executed dishes circulating through his medium-sized restaurant.

Diners assemble their meal—in our case, brunch—by

pointing to dishes on the passing carts, which are pushed along by Chinese women who announce the dish in Cantonese-accented English. These same ladies serve the dish, record the transaction in ink with the appropriate rubber stamp (called a 'chop') on the table's tab, and push on to the next table, all in one practiced series of tidy motions. While ambiance and service may have been perfected by the French, the Chinese focus strictly on the food. But, after many times of going to this particular restaurant, we have come to know a few little details about the Chinese women pushing the carts: one husky woman barks out the names of the dishes but smiles when the diners pick from her cart. Another has a jade bracelet that she offered to sell us once, when we pointed admiringly to it. She laughs about it again whenever we come in. Another asked Lauren a question in Mandarin, which allowed Lauren to say, "Oh, I'm not Chinese. I'm Japanese." This caused the questioner to pull back and say, "Ah," appraisingly. Another draws her pigtail from the side, instead of the back, of her long, straight hair, and impishly tries her English out on us. Another, whose name we think we heard as Ming-Deh, always asks in English if we want to make a special order for a particular item to be brought to us from the kitchen (which, we guess, costs a little bit more than the same item would cost if selected from the circulating carts). She seems to be a natural salesperson, with a friendly, open acceptance of her dining customers, an obvious intelligence, and a sincere desire to understand the American diners; not to just push carts past them on her shift.

We don't see Ming-Deh at the restaurant today, so we just settle for the extraordinary tastes of the exquisite dim sum served to us. And as we dine on this strange and beautiful food, in itself an exquisite way to mark the beginning of a memorable Thanksgiving, maybe we even dream a little that we may see a dragon suddenly walk through the front door.

After brunch, we go to Grace Cathedral on Nob Hill to walk the outside labyrinth, which is patterned after the 800-year-old labyrinth laid in the floor of Chartres Cathedral near Paris. Unlike a maze where the walker can easily get lost, the labyrinth leads its trekkers on a single, clear, switch-back path that inevitably arrives at the center, and then leads one back out again. The "purpose" or intent of the labyrinthine journey is a ritual of "releasing" on the walk in, receiving spiritual illumination in the center, and returning to the world on the walk out. Labyrinths have been constructed in various forms in all spiritual traditions throughout the world: one found near Galisteo, New Mexico, is reported to be over 3,500 years old.

Whenever Lauren and I enter the Grace Cathedral labyrinth, we always ask for "inner direction" on whatever is troubling us at the moment. Oftentimes, one or both of us get an inner answer somewhere on the path in, during a moment in the center, or on the path out. Whether we get an answer or not, we always benefit from the soothing of the soul that comes from inner focus on a walking meditation amidst the grand vistas from Nob Hill.

The rest of Wednesday afternoon is spent sightseeing, shopping, people watching, and just catching up on the newest styles that will, in two or three years, dominate fashion in our hometown 235 miles away. We check into our hotel and stop in the hotel lounge for late-afternoon tea, served by a friendly Chinese woman in her early thirties, whose name tag says "Linda."

"Do you want to go to the wine bar for appetizers instead of having dinner?" I ask Lauren.

Being close to the Napa and Sonoma valleys, San Francisco is a logical place to find America's best wines. But, being a city of inventive cuisine and entrepreneurial spirit, San Francisco also searches the world to find wines to compare and contrast with its own. To the typical local's mind, a wine can't be called "world class," unless it can compare favorably in a blind tasting, alongside the best other wines the world has to offer. The wine bars in Paris carry many good French wines, with a smattering of wines from other countries. The wine bars in San Francisco carry the best wines in the world, with the best domestic offerings competing on equal footing with the most distinguished wines from New Zealand, Spain, Italy, Argentina, and anywhere else bold enough to sell in the vigorous world-wide wine market. The best wine bars in other cities may typically have ten to fifteen different bottles open for tastes of wine. The best wine bar in San Francisco typically has sixty open bottles, with two ounce tastes arranged in flights of three to five similar wines, grown continents apart, or next door, or some combination that the sommelier finds interesting. What's new, interesting, or just different in wine this week can be sampled for a small price at this "emporium of purple passion."

"I don't want to drink too much," Lauren says, "maybe just one flight of sparkling wine."

"Okay, we could have some of the cheese appetizers with the wine."

Our favorite wine bar pairs cheese, nuts and fruit, and other appetizers with the flights of wine, thus emphasizing the special characteristics of the wine. This practice also renews the recurring wonder that something made of grapes can taste amazingly similar to something made of grapefruit, dates, nuts, figs, or any of the world's other fruits. *How do they do that?*

We pass a pleasant evening in the wine bar, listening

to live jazz music, trying wines from all over the world, talking about how the wines mesh with the appetizer accents, joking with the waiters, and generally enjoying the "life is good" feeling that always comes with this experience. As is our habit, we take a cab back to the hotel and fall into a conversation with the Anglo cab driver about how the night is "layered" for a typical San Francisco cabbie.

"The hip-hoppers take cabs between 5 and 7 in the morning, when their clubs close," the cabbie said. "The junkies and speed freaks go home between 2 and 5 in the morning. Drunks between midnight and 2 a.m. The prostitutes take cabs between 10 and 12."

"Don't you have any *regular* people as customers?"

"Sure, but all of the respectable people are off the streets by 10 p.m."

We all laugh, as we realize that it's 9:30 p.m. and that we've just been pigeonholed.

Thanksgiving morning: I get up at 6:00 a.m. and go to the hotel lobby to pick up coffee and apples, noting that the hotel has started to charge for the coffee, which used to be free. Back in the room, Lauren and I sip our drinks and talk about what to do for the day.

"I saw something in the hotel magazine that mentioned a wave organ at the Marina. There was also something about a stair walk from the Embarcadero up to Coit Tower, which might be interesting." Lauren said.

"Sounds like a good start to a Thanksgiving Day. Let's take the stair walk first, since it's closest, and go from there."

We drove over to the Embarcadero, San Francisco's waterfront district on the bay, which had blossomed after the 1989 Loma Prieta 7.1 earthquake damaged the adjacent elevated Embarcadero Freeway. To its credit, the city had replaced the freeway with a broad boulevard along the now-unobstructed bay front. We quickly found the concrete stairway mentioned in the hotel magazine and began to climb, pausing to turn and breathe in the sea air, while marveling at the panoramic views that expanded with each step up. Soon the stairway entered a common area behind the back-to-back houses on two adjacent streets. The walkway became a tree-shaded, wooden planked sidewalk, wedged between the backyards of the passing houses. The neighborhood we were walking through was very old (one of the oldest in San Francisco, we later learned), but very well maintained, with stunning views of Coit Tower and San Francisco Bay. At the last turn, before the neighborhood gave way to steep, concrete stairs ascending the rest of the way to Coit Tower, we suddenly heard a cackling in the air. Lauren and I turned to see a flock of about twenty birds wheel and land in the trees around us. Looking closer, we began to realize that these electric-green-bodied, cherry-headed birds were wild parrots. *How could wild parrots flourish in a metropolitan area surrounded by 7 million people?*

We later learned that the birds were actually large, red-masked parakeets, wild-caught in Ecuador or Peru, which had somehow escaped after being imported into San Francisco to be sold as pets in the 1980s. Today the birds are just our fellow pilgrims, enjoying their freedom on Thanksgiving Day. We laughed, and the birds took off; but we felt privileged to have seen such a rarity.

Lauren and I finish the climb to the top of Coit

Tower and silently take in the magnificent views of the Golden Gate Bridge, Alcatraz, the Bay Bridge, and the rest of San Francisco. We climb back down through the neighborhood, and pass charming, little-known neighborhood restaurants, each of which has its own spectacular views of the bay and its bridges.

Finding the car where we had left it at the bottom of the stairs, we drive toward the Marina. As we pass Ghiradelli Square, and are thankful that the tempting chocolate stores are not yet open, I see people swimming in the waters of Aquatic Park. "Let's go look!" I say to Lauren. We stop, walk out onto the semi-circular pier between Aquatic Park and Fort Mason, and stare in amazement at three older Caucasian men swimming in the Park's cold ocean waters. The air temperature is about 55 degrees Fahrenheit and we are wearing light jackets. One of the swimmers is not wearing a wet suit—invigorating exercise for Thanksgiving morning!

"Where was the wave organ you read about?" I ask Lauren.

"Somewhere at the end of a jetty that forms one side of the Marina. The article said that a group of artists used marble and granite stones from a demolished cemetery to create walks, benches, and platforms for 25 concrete and PVC pipes that make up the organ. The pipes are set at different elevations within the site. When the tide rises and falls, the lapping of the waves and the movement of the water in and out of the pipes is supposed to create sounds of different pitches. And that's the wave organ."

We drive to the Marina, park at the end of the jetty separating the Marina from San Francisco Bay, and walk along a dirt path on the top of the jetty out to the end. Sitting on one of the benches among the pipe ends, we listen intently, but neither of us can hear anything in particular.

"Maybe we should meditate," I said, "and then we might be able to hear the wave organ."

At first, we hear nothing. Then we become aware of the environment: the hard stone we're sitting on, the taste and smell of the sea air, the distant drift of sailboats, the cawing sea gulls, the far away urban sounds, and our own breathing. Slowly, we also become aware of the many distant fog horns around San Francisco Bay that are sounding their notes, all different and out of time, like an orchestra of tuba players warming up for a concert. Finally, we hear the gentle lapping of the waves against the pipe ends and the deep glug-glug sound of the water compressing and releasing within the pipes. We salute the creators of this subtle installation for making an art piece that is accessible only through contemplation.

"It's time for lunch," Lauren says. "Do you think anything will be open?" Since it is close by, we drive over to the Cliff House, San Francisco's Civil War era restaurant site, which faces the open ocean. Unfortunately, it's very crowded with diners seeking the "turkey with relatives" Thanksgiving experience, and we drive back to Union Square to LaScala in the 1920s styled Sir Francis Drake Hotel, only to find it closed for Thanksgiving.

"What about the St. Francis?" Lauren says. We walk over to the hotel (built in 1902 and rebuilt after the Great Quake of 1906) and stop at the dining room with its great, dark green granite pillars toward the front of the hotel and a full view of the giant Christmas tree on Union Square. They have just opened and are serving a Mediterranean lunch of hummus, babaganoush, lamb, and pita bread, perfect for the moment. This "Thanksgiving experience" continues to become increasingly magical, as we flow along with the moments leisurely presented to us and as we follow our feelings about what to "manifest" next.

"Let's walk a little bit in Chinatown," Lauren says, after we finish our late lunch.

Outside of the hotel, we take the cable car up Powell Street and get off on the outskirts of Chinatown at a particular spot where we've never been before. I turn to look in a shop window, and not an arm's length away in a metropolitan area of 7 million people, I suddenly see Ming-Deh, the waitress we missed the day before at the dim sum parlor, walking with her three-year old daughter. We greet, and she excitedly tells us in English and pantomime that, the Saturday before, she quit the dim sum parlor to open a small restaurant near where we are standing. We take the name of her new restaurant and promise to visit when it's open for business. With our experiences this morning and with this improbable meeting against all odds, we begin to get the feeling that the day is experiencing us, rather than us experiencing the day; and we gladly let it unfold.

Lauren begins to look in the Chinatown tourist shops, all of which seem to be open on Thanksgiving. Past the cheap souvenirs in one of the shops, Lauren suddenly sees a dark wooden kitchen implement holder in the shape of a bamboo stalk, resembling something we had seen once in a restaurant on a previous trip (and had been unable to find during many subsequent trips to San Francisco). It is a perfect design fit for our kitchen, and we marvel again at the day's serendipitous delights. We continue for the rest of the afternoon to walk and browse the sights of this compact city.

Thanksgiving dinner in the hotel is the only advance restaurant reservation we made for the trip; and when we arrive at the appointed time, we find ourselves being served by the other day's late-afternoon tea pourer, "Linda." Since it is early and the restaurant is nearly empty, Linda takes time to answer our questions about the new charge for morning coffee, the hotel's new Japanese owners, and the many service changes being made.

Lauren asks Linda, "How long have you lived here?"

Suddenly, Linda begins to tell us her whole amazing story. She was born in Calcutta, India, and grew up across the street from the Missionaries of Charity mission, where Mother Theresa worked. Her parents moved the family to Macao and then moved to San Francisco with the help of an uncle who had first established a family foothold in America. Four years ago, Linda returned to India for a visit. Because she had known Mother Theresa and her fellow missionaries in the old neighborhood, Linda went to pay her respects at the mission. The head missionary welcomed Linda, and after listening to her life story, asked Linda to return the next day. When Linda returned, the missionary introduced her to a two-month old baby girl who had been birthed at the mission. The baby's mother was Indian and her father from Nepal, which was a recipe for lifelong discrimination in caste-conscious Calcutta.

"Would you take the baby back to the United States

with you?" the missionary asked Linda.

Stunned, Linda called her parents in San Francisco and told them what the missionary had asked. They talked about it on the telephone for a long time: Linda was unmarried and working two jobs; so taking the baby would require a commitment from the whole family. But as they talked about the baby, their excitement grew, until they finally decided to say "yes." Linda informed the head missionary, the paperwork was quickly completed, and a new pilgrim returned to San Francisco with Linda.

Linda apologized for having let her story spill out to two complete strangers and said, "I am a private person and don't usually talk about my life." But on this Thanksgiving Day of openness to experience, we were probably the perfect ones to hear Linda's story.

We got up the next morning, retraced our drive back to San Luis Obispo, and reflected on this extraordinary Thanksgiving: the history of the Spanish, Chinese, Japanese, Portuguese, Swiss, and other ethnic migrations to California; the experience of our own families' past immigrations; the struggles of the entrepreneurial Ming-Deh; Linda's compassionate decision to bring up an immigrant baby in America; and even the startling sight of wild, free-flying parakeets—all of us thankful pilgrims manifesting our dreams in a bountiful land.

CHAPTER THIRTEEN

OH LORD, WON'T YOU BUY ME A MERCEDES-BENZ

"Our deepest fear is not that we are inadequate. Our deepest fear is that we are powerful beyond measure."—Marianne Williamson

SITTING ON THE SMOOTH LINOLEUM FLOOR in my mother's kitchen, I wound up the toy car with the mechanical key that had come with it, set the car flat on the floor, and slowly released my eight-year-old finger and thumb from the two rear wheels. Depending upon how I had set the control bar near the front headlights, the car would turn in tight circles, swoop around in wide circles, or zoom straight across the floor until the heavy internal spring uncoiled completely. The car was surprisingly hefty and never jittered or veered from its set course. It was also beautiful to look at, with its clean styling lines, excellent workmanship, metallic silver body, and solid feel. The model car was a present given to me by an uncle returning from military service overseas, and it was one of my favorite toys: sleek, durable, and made with an obvious commitment to excellence.

Now, more than fifty years later, I look back at my experience with that silver toy car and recognize that *something* important began for me back then...something I wouldn't clearly understand—or begin to value and *use*—until decades later, when I developed more clarity about how "manifestation" works.

You see, my sense is that most people, myself included, tend to follow the "role models" that happen to be in front of them in childhood, until any particular model shows itself (i.e., him/herself) to be inadequate for furthering one's growth or happiness or both. In my case, my father was my original role model, and he first bought *used* cars when I was young.

While he bought a variety of used makes and models back then, my *favorite* car he got when I was growing up was a used, white 1953 Cadillac. This particular old Cadillac severely tested my father's considerable skill at keeping mechanical objects running. However, it was a substantial, well-engineered vehicle with a ride that felt like the car's heavy mass was slipping along a well-oiled track, not bumping along like the rest of the cars on the country roads surrounding our house. Once, when my father was driving me to a dentist appointment, he let the engine out all the way on a straight stretch of freshly-paved two lane country road, only easing off on the gas pedal when the speedometer reached 100.

"Don't tell your mother," he said with a laugh, and we both enjoyed our secret conspiracy of power and speed.

The first new car my father bought when he could finally afford it was a stripped-to-the-bare-bones Studebaker that he paid cash for from savings. After that, my father bought a series of new, but inexpensive,

Chrysler products, always paying cash that he had saved up. And he was content with those purchases.

Those who interpret dreams oftentimes say that a dream about a car symbolizes you in your waking life, in your physical body. Thus, for example, if you've just had a dream about yourself driving in a shiny, red convertible, pleasantly going down a smooth, tree-lined road, it can symbolize that you're "driving" your life the right way, maintaining your body in good condition, and that you do not need any redirection.

I think that the relationship between our cars and our self-image goes further than just inhabiting our dreams—I think it subconsciously affects our whole lives and who we think we are. In looking back at the cars I bought over the years, I now realize that I was repeating patterns I learned as a child, with a twist along the way. My first cars were used Chrysler products (made by a manufacturer I was familiar with through my father's purchases); my first new car was a bare-bones Toyota Corona for family use (comparable to my father's first bare-bones Studebaker); but my first personal car, that I alone would drive, was a new, white Cadillac (like my father's, but new, and thus my first break from familiar automobile territory).

I often thought that the new white Cadillac symbolized what I thought I wanted to be at that time: big and bold. And in a certain way, I "manifested" that self-image via my purchase of that car. My white Cadillac lasted for 100,000 miles and then began to deteriorate mechanically. I bought another; but it was underpowered, less well engineered, not as stylish as the first, and was, I had to admit, somewhat gaudy. I was almost relieved when it was stolen and stripped, requiring the purchase of a new car.

What to buy? I was beginning to make more money, but how much could I justify spending on a new car? Somehow, I was drawn to a medium-sized black Mercedes Benz and couldn't resist its solid feel, tight European handling, and the way it made driving seem as though the car was an extension of my body in time and space. I put 142,000 miles on the "Black Pearl" before I decided that I needed another new car.

By this time, I had enough savings to pay cash for a new car. I went to the Mercedes dealer and looked over its offerings, but none seemed exactly right. As I was turning to leave, I saw a car-carrier truck transport pull into the dealership with a delivery of ten new cars. On the top row, the second car back from the front, was "my" car—a medium-sized silver Mercedes.

"Can I have that one?" I asked the salesman, pointing to the one on the truck.

"Just give us time to unload it, and it's yours."

They say that the way you get your money out of a luxury car that costs twice as much as other cars that can get you from point A to point B is to drive it until the wheels fall off, until the cost of repair and replacing dictates the need for a new car. I drove that silver Mercedes for 30,000 miles; but then I quit my lucrative job and moved to the country to write, working at my profession only part-time. No concern about a new car entered my mind until the silver Mercedes reached 110,000 miles. By then, I was in a position where I could not really afford to replace it when it got too expensive to maintain.

How do you go about getting something that you want that you can't afford? For many years, I had been a linear thinker, assuming that everyone got what they wanted by going after it, moving logically and according to a preset plan, step by step, toward eventually affording it, *making it happen*—hard work and all of that. But there were some things that I had gotten in my life by simply wanting them, by intending them, and then by stepping through the doors that suddenly opened to them. Becoming a lawyer had happened that way for me.

From an early age, I had wanted and intended to be a lawyer; but my family's modest financial circumstances suggested that it would never happen.

However, through scholarships, loans, and my refusal to let the dream die, it happened (although not in ways I ever expected). Perhaps most surprisingly, when I neared graduation from high school, my favorite uncle—who managed a specialty construction business—casually asked me one day what I thought about working with him one summer. I leaped at the chance, and that job paid well enough to meet my needs for the next eight summers. I should note that, in my family, graduating from high school meant you immediately became the sole source of funding for any living expenses, advanced education, or anything else. Working with my uncle also gave me the dignity of earning my own keep. Even I was amazed at how it had all happened—I had never met another person who had wanted to be a lawyer, who had no apparent means of getting there, but who nevertheless did get there by passionately wanting it and by seizing the opportunities that always seemed to come along. Was there a principle at work here? And if so, how would it best be described? Was it sheer luck? Or did I somehow make it happen in a way that I had never made anything happen before? Later in life, I framed the question in a different way, based upon much of what I'd studied in both science (specifically, quantum physics and human consciousness) and spirituality. Is "manifestation" through thought possible? In other words, can something be facilitated to show up in your life, simply because you want it or intend it to?

I had a vivid dream one night, during the period of my exploration of quantum physics and human consciousness. In the dream, I stopped to talk with a construction worker inside the ground floor of a poorly-lit, dirt-floored building under construction. He was operating a piece of heavy equipment (a crane), deftly and easily moving and positioning an impossibly huge pipe, which was shaped like a boat and filled with some construction material. He motioned for me to go outside, and once we were outside, he simply said: "Intention implies fulfillment."

When I awoke, I realized that what I had been told, rather directly, in the dream was really quite profound: we are creative beings; we are given the tools to accomplish any result we can imagine; we could not have imagined any result if we had not also been given the power to accomplish that result; and *our* part in the whole process is simply to form, express, and hold the intention. I felt assured by this dream that I could actually accomplish whatever purpose came to me, much like the famous Walt Disney remark: "If you can dream it, you can do it."

While most of the world currently looks at getting what you want as a linear process, maybe it isn't linear at all. Maybe it is simply human intention (or "desire consciousness") enthusiastically applied to the quantum field that produces any desired result. Because humans have long thought that the process of creation was linear, it unfolded in a linear manner. However, what if humans thought that the creative process could produce anything at all, so long as humans intended it? What if achieving results was like making movies—you can make any movie you choose to, and if you want a different result, you can just make a different movie? I had myself experienced the process of "creation"—like the realization of my dream of becoming a lawyer—in a way that had not occurred in a linear manner but had occurred through a series of improbable coincidences. How could intention be made to result in fulfillment in everyday life? Using the language of physics, how could quantum creation be accomplished practically?

I decided to study how what I am calling "manifestation"—having something that you think about actually show up in your life—in fact, worked; how "intention" could ultimately result in me getting something that I wanted. To study manifestation, I began creating a list on the first day of each New Year of all of the things I wanted to be, have, or do in the coming year. After creating my "be, have, or do" list, I would put it away and only look at it on the last day of the year. Time and time again, I was amazed at how many of the things I had wanted in the beginning of the year I had actually gotten by the end of that year. I then began maintaining a running manifestation list: whatever I wanted, I put on the list. Time and time again, what was on the list manifested in my life.

It should be noted that things *never* showed up in my life *exactly* how I thought they would, *and* I had to follow the little "suggestions," no matter how improbable, that would suddenly appear in my mind, in order to find the path to the items.

The only items that didn't seem to manifest were specific requests involving specific persons. For example, I could not make someone love me or resolve a quarrel. It was as if one intention alone could work wonders; but if two intentions were involved, they had to be aligned together to bring anything into being.

After reviewing the available literature on quantum physics and consciousness and comparing it to my own experience, I concluded that what made the manifestation process work best for me was not methodically grinding out the steps to my goal but simply focusing on my desire, expectancy, and belief about the item.

Desire involved knowing exactly what I wanted, with as much specificity and emotion as possible. Lauren and I once sat down and developed a three-page list of *exactly* what we wanted in a house we could afford. We wrote out the essence of what we wanted, as well as our very specific desires regarding location, acreage, landscape, design, rooms, and technology. We were delighted, and frankly surprised, when the "quantum field of all possibilities" delivered to us *exactly* the house we wanted *at a price we thought we could afford* (which was, of course, one of the specifics we listed).

"How is your day going?" is a question we often ask one other. What if I sat down and wrote out in as much detail as possible how I *wanted* my day to go, what my perfect day would consist of? I did so once, as an exercise, and then, to my great shock and delight, I had one. *Do you know what activities bring you joy? When is the last time you did any of them? Is anything stopping you from doing them?* When I asked myself these questions, obvious solutions appeared, and my real desires crystallized into form.

There was another essential component I discovered in desire: worthiness. *Am I entitled to have what I want? Is it wrong for a spiritually-minded person to want to drive a Mercedes-Benz? Is it crass materialism to call upon the power of the universe to produce a luxury automobile for me to drive?* Maybe.

On the other hand, the power of the universe seems to be impersonal: the sun shines its rays equally and without judgment on the world's humblest saint, on the world's biggest sinner, and on me. Gravity pulled just as hard on Buddha as it does on me. The Bible does not say, "Ask, and it will be given to you, unless 'it' is a Mercedes." There's a story told about Pope John Paul II, that he was once asked a negative question at an American news conference: could he explain why he had allowed church funds to be spent on building a new swimming pool at the Papal Summer Palace? His answer, "I like to swim. Next question."

No, it seems to me that, so long as it does not cause harm, you are worthy to desire whatever you want to desire; you are worthy to get it; and you are endowed with the means. The universe, I believe, deals with any crass materialism in our desires through Buddha's Second Noble Truth: the origin of suffering is attachment. The wonders of the universe are there for us to play with but not to become attached to. "Power tends to corrupt, and absolute power corrupts absolutely," because of the temptation to "lose oneself" or "give oneself over" to having the power. Love of wine can be a beautiful, sensual experience in this material world; but attachment to wine can lead to alcoholism, sickness, and death. The trick is to, as the Sufis say, "Be in the world, but not of it." So, yes, I believe that I am entitled to use the powers of the universe to buy me a Mercedes Benz, so long as I don't cry when it gets into an accident.

Expectancy, I discovered, had something to do with feeling that I deserved to have the thing I wanted and watching for opportunities to have it. I once attended a seminar where the exercise was to ask "the universe" to deliver something to you that you really wanted and to imagine that the universe could deliver it to you, no matter how much it cost. At the next session of the seminar, two months later, you were to tell what had happened to your request. I recall almost everyone making progress on receiving what they had asked for; that is, all except for one participant, who had wanted an expensive racing bicycle, but who said at the second session of the seminar: "Oh, I'll never be able to afford it." He could not accept the ground rule of the exercise, that price was to be no object. His expectancy was that he could only have what he could afford, not what he wanted; and he, thus, made no progress in getting it.

I had a thrifty friend, who for a long period in his early life, had habitually frequented fast food restaurants but frequently complained afterward about feeling tired or "bogged down." Once, when traveling with a companion to a large nearby city, the companion suggested having lunch in the best restaurant in town.

When my thrifty friend asked why, the companion said: "Someone has to eat in the best restaurant in town; it might as well be us." On that day, my thrifty friend stopped eating in fast food restaurants and found that even the best restaurant in town always had something that he wanted to eat at a price he felt comfortable with.

If I need a parking space in order to attend a concert, why not pull up and look for the parking space directly in front of the concert hall, instead of starting to look four blocks away?

Belief for me only has to be 51% for manifestation to work. Anything less than that tells me that I really don't believe that it will happen, and so it won't. I get to at least 51% believing that something will happen by reviewing other things that I wanted, which I wasn't sure could happen, but that did happen. As I'd mentioned previously, becoming a lawyer from unlikely circumstances is a prime example; so is getting a perfect house I could afford or getting preferred parking spaces 99% of the time. And oh yeah, let's not forget getting *all* of the items on my "be, have, and do" lists and having "perfect" days manifest, *just as I'd intended them.*

But would my theory work on manifesting a new Mercedes? The model I wanted would require an extra $55,000 in cash, or an extra $80,000 in income with the tax due figured in. Where is that going to come from, I asked myself, when I'm working part-time and just covering ongoing expenses? On the other hand, someone's got to drive those cars, so it might as well be me. Since I'm close to the 51% minimum belief level, I'm thinking that this might take a while and that I could use all of the help I could get.

At about that time, I became interested in *feng shui* and the power of having symbols around that represent things that I want to have happen in my life. *What symbol could I use for the Mercedes I want?* I wondered. As soon as I asked myself the question, the idea immediately occurred to me that toy manufacturers often make small scale models of many current automobiles. *Why do they do that? I wondered. Who buys the models? Only children? Do other people use symbols to help their subconscious reach into the quantum field and turn the levers that produce what they intend?*

The feeling suddenly came, "Let's find out!" I quickly located a toy store that had *exactly* the silver model Mercedes that I wanted. I bought the five-inch long model and put it on top of my computer case, where I would see it every time I turned my computer on or off.

There the little toy sat for the next two years, while my current car's odometer reached 160,000, 180,000, 200,000 miles, and the repair bills began to climb. I thought about other options and different cars but finally determined to hold the intention and see what happened. In the third year, I had the strong feeling one day to call a client with whom I had lost touch. He immediately responded with a request to do more work, which ultimately resulted in a $20,000 increase in my income for that year. In preparing for my year-end taxes, the accountant casually mentioned that this was the last year that the entire cost of a business automobile could be written off in the first year as new equipment—meaning that $20,000, otherwise due in income tax, was suddenly available to go towards the purchase of the car. One of Lauren's nephews had gotten a great price from an online car purchasing service, so I got in touch with the service and realized that I could have the car I wanted for $5,000 less than I had expected! Because I was within striking distance of my financial goal, and my current car odometer read 222,222, I went ahead and ordered the Mercedes, even if I would have to finance part of it. At the end of the year, the company I was working with declared a $35,000 bonus for all who had contributed to the company's success that year. Suddenly, there was the $80,000 I needed to fully pay for my new Mercedes and to pay the tax on the extra income used to purchase the car.

A few weeks after I took delivery of the Mercedes, I was turning on my computer one day when my eyes abruptly focused on the little silver model Mercedes sitting on the computer case. In amazement, I realized it looked exactly like the full-sized silver Mercedes sitting in my garage; so much so that I was moved to photograph the new car with the uncannily-similar toy model sitting on its roof.

As I look at the photographs of the small symbol sitting atop the larger manifestation, I suddenly remembered the smooth linoleum floor in my mother's kitchen and realized that the heavy, silver model car that had raced along that floor and into my intentions fifty years ago *must* have been a silver Mercedes Benz sedan, like the one now sitting manifest in my driveway.

Oh, I should mention: I later gave the little silver model to Lauren, and after solemnly putting out the intention and applying the manifestation principles we had learned, she soon and serendipitously, almost accidentally, got a "big" one too.

CHAPTER FOURTEEN

A HAPPY ACCIDENT

"There is no such thing as accident; it is fate misnamed."—*Napoleon Bonaparte*

"Angels, please protect the car and everyone in it today," Lauren said as we rolled from the garage towards the gate, thus beginning our three-and-a-half hour drive to San Francisco.

"Whoa, where's that coming from? You don't usually say things like that."

"I just had the feeling to surround the car with white light and to say it out loud."

"Oh."

Six months earlier a psychic had told me that I would have an accident when I least expected it. *Is today the day?* I wondered. *Should I cancel the trip because of Lauren's premonition?* After a moment's reflection, I ended up thinking, *Not at all.* Psychics have been wrong before, and fear is no way to live. Besides, I believe that information about the future is presented to me, *not* so that I can avoid life situations, but so that I can be ready for what comes when it comes *and* so that I can simply make the best of it, without undue emotion.

Que sera, sera, I muse to myself. Besides, the day is sunny, 68 degrees, and it always refreshes my spirit to drive through the Salinas Valley and see the partnership man has entered with Nature to produce the cornucopia of fruits and vegetables pouring daily from that fertile land.

Lauren and I drive and chat for awhile and then enjoy the comfortable silence, back and forth like that, while we gaze out at the beauty of the surrounding panorama. As we approach San Francisco, I take a less-trafficked route that skirts heavily-urbanized San Jose, and is laid out along coastal mountains clothed in redwood forest, with ocean fog curling inland over the peaks.

I start to make the transition from Highway 85 to the 280 freeway, and I concentrate because this particular transition is complicated. The two-lane on-ramp from 85 first merges with four lanes of the 280, then becomes an off-ramp to the Foothill Expressway, and then disappears—all in the space of about a quarter of a mile.

As we approach, a driver is maneuvering from the far left lane of the 280, across four lanes of seventy-five-miles-per-hour traffic, onto the two-lane off-ramp. To accomplish it, the driver slows way down, and other cars brake, slow down, and swerve to avoid hitting this exiting car, as do I. Suddenly, the exiting driver is not just slowing down, but is now braking hard. Several cars behind the exiting driver, including me, brake hard too, and at that moment, I hear and feel the sickening crunch from behind: *I've been hit!*

But the traffic pattern is still in chaos, and I keep focus on the pattern, lest I become involved in more collisions. I don't even dare break concentration to look to see what vehicle had hit me.

As I pull off the freeway, my mind races to conclusions—any substantial tap to a car's body, and this one was substantial, will cost at least $1,000 to fix, which I'll probably have to pay (with a $500 deductible, it's better to pay the $1,000 than to file a claim and have future insurance rates raised). The driver of the other car is probably lost in the confusion and long gone on the 280 freeway. However, pulling to a stop on the shoulder, I check the rear view mirror for approaching traffic, and, to my amazement, I see a car pulling in behind me.

I get out and inspect the damage to my car—just as I thought, $1,000 worth. Still, the damage is not too bad and will not hinder our San Francisco weekend: Monday is soon enough to deal with the fix. And if they have to repaint the bumper, they'll probably have to paint the entire bumper to get the color uniform, which would entail painting the other scratches out (including the spider web pattern where months ago someone apparently scraped a box along the top of the bumper near the trunk lid). *Hmmm...maybe there's an upside here*, I speculate.

Lauren gets out of the car but wisely stays in the background, not wanting to add energy one way or the other to what's about to unfold. I look at the other car—a late-model, less expensive Mercedes Benz—and the driver, a teenager, who's now busy dialing a number into his cell phone. *Calling his parents, no doubt*, I think to myself. Still, I am surprised and impressed that he stopped and let himself in for whatever grief would undoubtedly come his way over an accident that would no doubt be deemed his fault. *And*, by stopping, I know that he has just saved me $1,000 because he or his insurance company would likely be responsible for fixing the damage to my car.

Still impressed that he had stopped at all, I walk over to him and say, "Good morning." He nods, but can't talk because he's still on the cell phone, getting, no doubt, last minute instructions from whomever is on the other end about exchanging information, not admitting liability, "Why weren't you paying attention!" etc. So, I go get my digital camera and busy myself with taking pictures of the damage to my car, the damage to his car, and him standing next to his car (mop of hair, T-shirt, plaid shorts worn low, Puma sneakers, no socks—a pleasant looking fellow, probably 17 or 18 years old). While I'm taking the pictures, the thought occurs to me: *How would the Walters in my life, either my uncle*

Walter or my friend Walter, have handled this situation? Both probably gently, I think.

When the cell phone call is over and the pictures are taken, I walk up and hand him a business card with my information on it. "Do you have a business card?" realizing as soon as I ask the question that teenagers don't carry business cards.

"No."

"Well, we can just write out the information."

He looks at the damage to his car, then to my car. As I start to write out his information, he says: "It's my father's car."

I smile, thinking *that's just what a father wants to hear at work at 10:30 on a Friday morning: "Hi, Dad! I just got into a wreck with your car."*

He hands me a card with his insurance agent's information, and I note that it's a notoriously stingy national insurer. Still, they would undoubtedly pay something. I feel for the teenager because I'm sure he's going to hear that the damage to both cars will cost his father at least $2,000.

The teenager says nothing about the accident. *Following instructions*, I silently say to myself. *Good for him*. He doesn't look scared or belligerent, just cautious, going through this required exercise with attention—good again.

Information exchanged, the teenager stands and looks at me, as if waiting for me to excuse him from the table he has just set, or more specifically, from any suggestion of "hit and run." I try to think of something witty to say to release him, but I think it may just come off as sarcastic. At that moment, I get the strong feeling to just shake his hand. I check with my intuition, my inner voice, for a fraction of a second and get the feeling that it's right. So, I extend my hand, which he takes, and suddenly there's no age gap there, no animosity or blame, no wariness in anticipation of a lecture…just a genuine smile.

We get into our respective vehicles and drive off.

"Thank the angels that it was not bad," Lauren says, and I do. This young fellow could *easily* have hit us at 75 miles per hour, not the 20 or so that he actually did, *and* the collision could have spiraled in an instant to involve other vehicles, which *were* traveling at 75 miles per hour.

It makes me think about the many other times that something has protected us, saving us from certain catastrophe: like the time I fell from a tree as a child and would have broken my neck in the fork of the trunk, except that my feet hit the ground a fraction of a second earlier; or the time as a child I was playing with my brother, when a pointed stick I threw toward him hit his cheek a safe half-inch below his left eye; or the time when Annie's car spun on a crowded freeway in Seattle, avoiding the passing cars and the 30-foot embankment; or when Lauren spun around several times off her side of the freeway completely, straight into the opposite lanes of oncoming traffic; or the time when Uncle Walter hit the button on the fire extinguisher and quenched the spark a millisecond before it ignited an explosion in the industrial paint booth we were standing in; or the time when the commercial airplane I was riding in was struck by lightning, and the engines suddenly went quiet but "miraculously" restarted two seconds later.

I shrug this "accident" off, remembering that one of the best days of my life, when I was falling in love with Lauren (again, twenty years after "the mirror image"), began with a drained battery that required waiting around for a recharge from the service people. So, I decide to forget about the fender-bender until Monday, and to just enjoy the weekend in San Francisco.

On Monday, the body shop confirms the $1,000 damage estimate. That afternoon, the telephone rings. "Hello, I'm Daniel's mother. There was an accident with my son on Friday. We've called our insurance company, and they'll be in touch with you about fixing your car. When he described the accident, he said that you were the nicest man about it. I just wanted to call to thank you for being so very nice to my son."

Wow, a mother calling to thank me for not being mean to her son! "Thank you for calling, but it just impressed me that he stopped. He didn't have to, and no one would ever have known."

"We try to teach our children values. Dealing with teenagers—sometimes it drives me crazy."

I think, *She's talking about her boy, but I had met the man.*

"When it happened, it just seemed to me to be one of those situations in life where a young man is presented with a choice, and your son made a good one. I'm not sure what I would have done at his age in that situation."

"Eight or nine months ago someone did that to him—hit his car on the freeway and just drove on. So he knows how that feels."

"Well, he sure got that lesson. Thanks again for calling."

A few days later, the telephone rings with *another* related caller on the other line. "Hi. This is David from the insurance company. I went to college in your town, and I loved it there. I want to tell you that we'll be taking care of the damage. All you have to do is take the car into our appraiser—it only takes half an hour. In fact, you can do that today. Our appraiser is only there one day a week, and this is the day. So it'll have to be today or a week from today. We'll supply a rental car for the time your car is being repaired. No one was hurt in the accident, right?

"David, I thought this was going to be easy. I have a written estimate from a reputable body shop and pictures of the damage, which I will e-mail you when our call is finished. I'm busy today. If you pay my body shop for the damage to my car without a hassle, I won't be needing a rental car during the fix, and we won't be complaining about being hurt in the accident. On the other hand, if you want me to jump through insurance company hoops...."

"Well, let me see if I can get the appraisal waived."

Which, of course, he did. The body shop did its usual beautiful job, including painting away the spider web pattern in the bumper paint near the trunk lid. When I went to the body shop to pick up the car, the estimator said, "I really enjoyed working with you on fixing this, particularly your sense of humor." I had the feeling that she meant it, that it wasn't just sales or future business development. Curiously, I didn't remember being particularly funny in dealing with the estimator: the accident business must be a grouchy one.

The entire experience had been a "positive" one: maybe the angels did protect us from more serious injury; it was gratifying to see a young man make the right choice under stress; the accident didn't interfere with a marvelous weekend in San Francisco; how sweet is it to have a mother call to thank you for not being mean to her son; the insurance company "took my word for it"; the body shop enjoyed the experience; and the fix removed the new and old unsightly scratches and dings to my bumper.

Why did it all happen this way? Was it because no one put any negative energy into the transaction? Was it because, throughout the whole experience, everyone used their intuition to deal with the "reality" at hand and to manifest a good result in the best interests of all concerned? Was it because everyone managed their fears: me about the cost of the repair; the other driver about the consequences; the insurance company about trusting claimants; and the body shop about potentially grumpy customers? I do not know; but in the end, to my complete surprise, I actually felt fortunate to have been given this experience of a happy accident.

CLOSING

A STEP-BY-STEP GUIDE TO USING THE THREE LAWS

"To each his own."—*Cicero*

IN THE OPENING STATEMENT, I asked you to:

1. read the fourteen stories in this book that chronicle transformative, awakening moments in my life;

2. try practicing the short exercises in this Closing—all of which are aimed to develop your fluency with the universal laws of intuition, manifestation, and healing; and,

3. then (i.e., *after* practicing the exercises), judge for yourself whether using the three laws described in this book leads you to a life in which: a) your most heartfelt desires start to crystallize for you, b) you begin to manifest these "dreams" into reality, and c) healing becomes more commonplace in your life.

I've attempted, below, to make an easy-to-follow, step-by-step guide to the three universal laws you've just read about—in the preceding fourteen stories—such that you would more readily know how to practically apply these laws in your daily life, whether at home, at work, or in the world at large.

Note that as the creator of your own reality, you shape your own version of the practice of the three laws. The magic of self-government is that if your practice of a universal law is not working for you, you can keep changing your practice until the law *does* work for you. This is not to say that you can change *other* universal laws—the law of gravity, for example—to suit you and your needs. But as you begin using *these* three laws, you'll likely discover there's some "flexibility" built into the effective practice of them, which can work to suit your own unique requirements. In other words, each person's practice of these particular universal laws is as individual as fingerprints or DNA. Part of that unique relationship is that you instinctively know better than anyone else what practice will best work to deliver to you the benefits of universal law. I can help you get started by showing you the template of what worked best for me, and then you can create what will work best for you. Here we go!

The Law of Intuition

"Your ears shall hear a word behind you, saying 'This is the way, walk in it...'"—*Isaiah 30:21*

You can actively use your intuition to get answers to your most pressing questions. How? The detailed steps I follow to get useful answers from my intuition are discussed at length in my book, *Ask Your Inner Voice*. Here is a summary of those steps:

Know that you are worthy to hear.

Accept the fact that you have been blessed with a subtle, yet powerful, channel to inner wisdom, your intuition; that useful thoughts or feelings have come to you, from time to time, throughout your life; and that they will come again.

Formulate a question.

Write out a question that states the essence of your dilemma or challenge (i.e., the choice you're facing) and that can be answered "yes" or "no." As in a successful Google search, the most effective questions are non-assuming, unambiguous, objective, specific, and complete. "Do I take this job?" Take as much emotion out of the question as possible.

Quiet the mind.

Take the question to a quiet place where you won't be disturbed and ask it mentally. Meditate, take a walk, sit by the water, lie in bed, or take a shower; and then ask your question. You will get better at accessing intuition the more you work with it. Eventually, you will be able to access it at any time. Including during a holdup.

Ask your question expecting an answer.

Be poised to hear and learn. Anticipate a fulfilling result. Let go of thoughts like, "This is a ridiculous exercise; I'll never get any answers this way; I should know better." Tap the fire of desire in looking forward to a successful outcome, an intuitive experience that will help with your dilemma or challenge.

Listen intently and patiently.

Think fishing: you put the bait out, you relax, you let your mind wander, and you wait for a nibble. It may come as words, a feeling, a "knowing," a mental picture, or anything that comes to you in the same or a similar way as your other thoughts normally do.

Pay attention to whatever you get.

The answer may seem too simple to be true or too obvious (as the truth often is); however, by earnestly reflecting on whatever comes forward, you might discover, in time, the relevance, usefulness, and profundity of your intuition's response.

Write down your answer.

Intuition's words may seem so simple, so mundane; they may be easy to forget. Write them down exactly as they come and look at them later to see how significant and meaningful they really are.

Act on your answer.

Satisfy yourself through appropriate discernment tests that the answer you received was guidance gained through a valid, universal channel. When you are satisfied, *act* on what you received. The only way you can learn to trust your intuition is by acting on it and observing that the consequences are beneficial. The only way your intuition can trust *you* is by learning from experience that you will consistently ask your dilemma/challenge questions *and* that you will act on the advice given.

The Law of Manifestation

*"...you got to have a dream,
if you don't have a dream,
How you gonna have a dream come true?"
—Rogers & Hammerstein, composers: "Happy Talk,"
from the musical* South Pacific

How can I get what I want? Here are the steps that work for me:

What do I really want?

Write out what you want to be, have, or do...*and why* you want such. The formulation may surprise you—do you really want $80,000 to buy a new car, or is what you *really* want the new car, even if it only costs you $20,000 or nothing at all? Which model? What features? What color? When you have finished writing out what you want, *in as much detail as possible*, ask your intuition if this is what you really want (see preceding steps for the "Law of Intuition").

Declare the intention to have what you want.

When you know what you really want to be, have, or do, declare that you want it, leaving "how is it going to happen" to universal law. Say it out loud. Place a symbol of what you really want—a toy model, a picture, a phrase—in a place where you will see it regularly.

Put the fire of desire into what you require.

See yourself *having* what you have declared that you want. Verify to yourself that you are worthy enough to have it. Envision yourself—using as many of your senses as possible—enjoying the feeling of having it. Make it come alive in your imagination *and* in your heart!

Expect to get it.

Don't take yourself out of the "receiving line" by negative thinking. Be open to the possibility of having what you want. *Someone's* got to have it: *it might as well be you.* Be ready for the subtle hunches and prompts that pop into your mind about ways to get what you want. Pay particular attention to any little suggestion or assistance that appears to be out of time sequence, like when an opportunity comes along to acquire free garage space for the car you want, *before* you actually have the car. Cooperate with serendipity.

Believe that you will get it.

Is there any way conceivable to me that I could get what I want? For example, if I want a parking space on the busiest street in the city, is there any way I can imagine that I *could* make that happen? Could I circle the block for hours until a space opened up? Could I look for a space at 3 a.m.? Could I pay a garage owner on the street a small fee to let me park in front of his driveway? If I know that I can get what I want by doing something completely out of proportion to the objective, I know that I can also get what I want in some unforeseen way; that is, I can choose to simply believe that the universe can deliver it to me in another, easier way. (And in thinking about conceivable ways to get what they want, people often come up with easy ways to get what they want and then just go do it, without invoking universal law any further.)

Let it go.

Think fishing again: Don't become so attached to the result of catching your fish that you scare the fish away. Let universal law do its work. Relax, do the next right thing that's been placed in front of you to do, and leave the results (including the timing) to the universe.

The Law of Healing

"Eventually you will come to understand that love heals everything, and love is all there is."—*Gary Zukav*

How to heal any person, place, or thing? Entire professions, countless books, and millions of people since the dawn of time have delved into this question. Through this collective experience, mankind has developed the science of medicine as its approved approach to human diagnosis and treatment; therefore, always consult a medical doctor first about the healing of any person, including yourself. As a *complement* to medical treatment, however, here are some steps that have worked for me:

Have faith.

Throughout history, some people have found ways to be an instrument of healing. The literature of all cultures and religions is replete with stories of healing. If faith the size of a mustard seed can move mountains, what might you accomplish if you are willing to invest a little faith in your power to facilitate healing?

A nonreligious, easy to follow description of how to heal may be found in Nina Paul's *Reiki for Dummies*, Wiley Publishing, Inc., 2006. A much more comprehensive study of alternative healing may be found in Barbara Brennan's *Hands of Light: A Guide to Healing Through the Human Energy Field*, Bantam, 1988.

What is your intention?

What are you trying to accomplish? What is your expectancy about the result? Your belief? Have you put the fire of desire into your intention? Get a clear focus of your intention through quiet contemplation or meditation.

If you feel yourself judging the person, place, or thing to be healed, consciously intend to let your feelings of judgment go as you prepare to express your intention for healing.

Many have found loving, compassionate action *with detachment* to be an appropriate attitude when working with healing. Such loving action is not invested in "fixing" or "rescuing" outcomes.

A comprehensive discussion of the scientific evidence regarding the effective use of human intention may be found in Lynne McTaggart's *The Intention Experiment*, Simon & Schuster, 2007.

What is the intention of the person requesting the healing?

Not everyone wants to be healed of their ailments. Some healing practitioners believe that they should be asked for healing assistance by the one to be healed *before* any healing is attempted.

What specific result is desired by the person requesting the healing? In general, focus on the person's receiving what *they* specifically want rather than on what *you* want for them. Seek to align your intention for the result of the healing with the result intended by the person to be healed.

What is the body saying?

Many believe that our bodies are sensitive instruments that tell us what to change, so as to bring our bodies back into healthy balance. But how to read the signals? Asking your intuition what a body is trying to tell its occupant about healing change is a good place to start (see preceding steps for the "Law of Intuition"). A comprehensive list of what the body may be saying through specific illnesses can be found in Louise Hay's *You Can Heal Your Life*, Hay House, 1999.

Is there anything your intuition tells you to share with the person requesting the healing, about the cause of the discomfort or how to heal it? Be sure to convey such in a simple, direct manner, conveying what you received from your intuition as purely as possible.

Touch

Many healers believe in laying hands on the body of the person to be healed. I believe it would be essential, first, to ask for permission to do this. Many others hold their hands a few inches above the place to be healed during the healing ceremony. Ask your intuition which is best for this person, at this time.

Forgiveness

Heartfelt forgiveness and love are integral to the healing of any relationship. Every perception of having been "wronged" alerts all participants in a relationship to an imbalance *and* to an opportunity to choose balance, wholeness, and love for the relationship going forward. The choice of forgiveness by all participants in a relationship is a vital step in the healing of that relationship. However, it's important to recognize no one can force or coerce another into forgiveness. Each must come to it at their own pace and in their own time.

The Healing Ceremony

The physical, mental, and spiritual setting you choose for healing can play an important role in the healing ceremony. Many prefer a quiet place, a meditative posture, and a shared intention between the healer and the person requesting the healing.

Visualize the person, place, or thing as actually healed in the current moment. Feel your own forgiveness, compassion, and love rising up for the person, place, or thing to be healed.

Again, *you* get to write the law of healing that works best for you. Here's a healing phrase (or affirmation) that, in my experience, has stopped colds, repaired damaged tissue, healed broken bones, lifted depression, and provided an abundance of supportive, healing energy: "I am perfect love, health, and happiness, in [whatever you believe is the source of the healing power—Spirit, the Universe, Love], for the body, mind and spirit of [the person, place, or thing to be healed] in the best interests of all concerned. So be it." Your own formulation of the law of healing can be used to heal yourself or another.

Feel gratitude for the healing, and let it go.

BIBLIOGRAPHY

Brennan, Barbara. *Hands of Light: A Guide to Healing Through the Human Energy Field.* New York, Bantam, 1988.

Cameron, Julia. *The Artist's Way.* New York: Putnam Berkley, 1992.

Choquette, Sonia. *Ask Your Guides: Connecting to Your Divine Support System.* Carlsbad, Ca.: Hay House, 2006.

Crary, Robert Wall. *The Still Small Voice.* Cleveland: Rishis Institute of Metaphysics, 1987.

Crum, Jessie K. *The Art of Inner Listening.* Los Angeles: Theosophical Publishing House, 1975.

Findhorn Foundation. *The Findhorn Garden.* Findhorn, Scotland: The Findhorn Foundation, 1975.

Guiley, Rosemary Ellen. *Harper's Encyclopedia of Mystical & Paranormal Experience.* New York: HarperCollins, 1991.

Hay, Louise. *You Can Heal Your Life.* Carlsbad, Ca.: Hay House, 1999.

Holmes, Ernest. *Science of Mind.* New York: Putnam Publishing Group, 1989.

James, William. *The Varieties of Religious Experience* (New York: The Modern Library, 1902)

McTaggart, Lynne. *The Intention Experiment: Using Your Thoughts to Change Your Life and the World.* New York: Free Press, 2007.

Merton, Thomas. *New Seeds of Contemplation.* New York: New Directions, 1961.

Mundy, Jon. *Listening to Your Inner Guide.* New York: Crossroad Classic, 1995.

Paul, Nina. *Reiki for Dummies.* New York: Wiley Publishing, Inc., 2006.

Robinson, Lynn A. *Divine Intuition: Your Guide to Creating a Life You Love.* New York: Dorling Kindersley Publishing, 2001.

Seale, A. *Intuitive Living: A Sacred Path.* San Francisco: Red Wheel/Weiser, 2001.

Spalding, Baird T. *Life and Teachings of the Masters of the Far East.* Marina Del Rey, Ca.: DeVorss & Co., 1924.

Sanders, C.W. *The Inner Voice.* Punjab, India: Radha Soami Satsang Beas, 1948.

Shumsky, Susan G. *Divine Revelation.* New York: Fireside, 1996.

Shumsky, Susan G., *How to Hear the Voice of God.* Franklin Lakes, N.J.: New Page Books, 2008.

Urantia Foundation. *The Urantia Book.* Chicago: 1955.

Walsch, Neale Donald. *Conversations With God.* New York: Putnam Berkley, 1997.

Wawro, James. *Ask Your Inner Voice*. Huntsville, AR: Ozark Mountain Publishing, 2010.

Yogananda, Paramhansa. *Autobiography of a Yogi*. Los Angeles: Self-Realization Fellowship, 1981.

ACKNOWLEDGMENTS

I WOULD LIKE TO THANK MY EDITORS, Willy Mathes and Tom Cannon, who reminded me once again of the powerful synergy that other minds bring to any writing. They patiently read every word, thought through every idea, and considered every sentence as a new reader would.

A special thanks is due all of the people in my life that helped me mature in age and grace in the celestial university in which we find ourselves: the armed robber who tested my faith in the Inner Voice; the women who plumbed with me the depths of loving thy neighbor; the professional colleagues who made the game interesting, especially the ones who helped me when they didn't have to: Jack Lewis, Roy Reardon, Elmer Stone, Bill Fenwick, John Lewis, and Tony Russo; Sonny, who taught me how to live with flaws; Walter Haswell, who taught me when it was time to awaken; Crystal Chuse, who taught the concept of the GodSelf to so many; my parents, whose *laissez faire* approach to their children's dreams taught that the harder the tests we devise for ourselves the more we become who we really are; my beloved son Jason Wawro; my sister Kathleen Decker and my brothers Mark, Dan, and especially Mike, the best friend I ever had; and finally my wife Lauren Eto, who after nearly forty years of togetherness, separation, and marriage still responds with love when I ask her to read a new paragraph I've just written.

ABOUT THE AUTHOR

JIM WAWRO, traditionally published author (*Ask Your Inner Voice*), executive coach, and former senior partner in a 1,400-lawyer firm, discovered while trying cases that some people have learned the secret to actively calling on their own intuition whenever they need it. Jim blogs at www.ActivateIntuition.com about proven methods of using intuition to dramatically improve the quality of your personal and professional life.

ALSO BY THE AUTHOR

Ask Your Inner Voice

Sometimes, words come up from very deep within us. Somehow, we can sense they are different from our other thoughts. They may come in the form of an instruction or a phrase of special wisdom. If we heed them, ensuing events always prove how absolutely right these words were. What would it be like to regularly have such inspiration appear just when you need it? What if you could easily receive strong and accurate inner guidance on the important decisions in your life, like decisions about career changes, relationships, and financial matters? How much fun would it be to have an inner voice that you trusted on everyday decisions and to have it lead you with coincidence and serendipity to exactly where you wanted to be in life? How satisfying would it be for your inner wisdom to guide you to immediate and lasting improvements in your relationships? All of that can be yours. Ask Your Inner Voice lays out the simple secrets people throughout history, and people alive today, have learned to use to call on their inner voice just when they need it. Ask Your Inner Voice shows through true inner voice stories the proven steps to connecting with your inner wisdom, and each chapter ends with a 'How To' section providing simple, 'Try It' exercises that you can use to tap into those aspects of your own inner voice.

The Best Wine Ever

Why do people drink wine?

Throughout history people have extolled the virtues of wine, but what is it about wine that inspires an emotional response that other historical spirits, like beer, simply do not?

Through forty years of experiencing and reading about the enjoyment of wine, I don't think that I have ever read anything that adequately explains why people enjoy wine so much. So I have attempted to capture the essence of the wine experience by touching on culture, law, human relationships, intuition, and great wines through the 2,200 words in this article.

Wine Enthusiast Magazine liked this explanation well enough to publish an excerpt of it as the last page of its December 15 issue.

I hope you enjoy reading my explanation of the best wine ever as much as I enjoyed researching it.

Right on the Money

"How much is this going to cost me?"—a question every client asks and every lawyer answers during the course of every litigated matter. Yet one of law's persistent mysteries is how to accurately estimate the attorneys' fees necessary to resolve a particular dispute.

But accurate estimates of anticipated attorneys' fees flow naturally and easily from the simple case analysis outlined with clarity in this 2,150-word article.

You will learn in this succinct article how to analyze the steps necessary to resolve any litigated dispute, how to evaluate the difficulty likely to be encountered at each step, how to gauge the likely overall litigation strategy of the other side, and how to thus calculate an accurate "bottom line" for almost any litigated matter.

The author brings to this subject successful experience as an associate in a Wall Street law firm, a founder of an AV-rated firm, a freelancer, an administrative partner for a 300-lawyer Silicon Valley firm, and a senior partner managing a 50-lawyer department in a 1,400-lawyer mega-firm. As such, the author has rendered, reviewed, paid, litigated, or arbitrated thousands of bills for attorneys' fees in the context of virtually every type of litigated matter and practice situation.

Little is written about how to accurately estimate anticipated legal fees in any particular litigated matter. This article provides specific, easy to apply guidelines for accurately evaluating the key factors to resolving any litigated dispute at a worth and cost acceptable to both lawyer and client.

Ask Your Inner Voice: How to Sell to Your Market

"Nothing happens until somebody sells something." And if you're like most, you may someday find yourself in the position of having to sell something. But if you're not a sales professional, how do you go about doing that exactly?

There are countless texts, videos, and audio presentations about how to sell—but they are all general. How do you go about selling the specific something that you have to sell?

In this delightfully short, 1,000-word article, you will learn, through the true story of an author faced with the task of selling a book, how to research what you need to know to sell anything, how to get the expert marketing help you require (at a price you can afford), how to condense all of the selling advice you receive into a workable marketing plan specific to what you are selling, and most importantly, how to use your own inner voice to guide you to marketing hits instead of marketing misses.

The author brings to this subject successful experience as a senior partner responsible for business development in a 1,400-lawyer firm and as the author of several books, including *Ask Your Inner Voice*, a definitive guide to proven methods for tapping into the wisdom that lies within you.

Little is written about how to tailor general marketing concepts to your specific marketing needs. Through the telling of a true story, this article provides specific, easy to follow steps for using your own inner voice to guide you to marketing success.

www.ingramcontent.com/pod-product-compliance
Lightning Source LLC
LaVergne TN
LVHW051117080426
835510LV00018B/2086